A New Economy?

THE CHANGING ROLE OF INNOVATION AND INFORMATION TECHNOLOGY IN GROWTH

OECD

ORGANISATION FOR ECONOMIC CO-OPERATION AND DEVELOPMENT

ORGANISATION FOR ECONOMIC CO-OPERATION AND DEVELOPMENT

Pursuant to Article 1 of the Convention signed in Paris on 14th December 1960, and which came into force on 30th September 1961, the Organisation for Economic Co-operation and Development (OECD) shall promote policies designed:

- to achieve the highest sustainable economic growth and employment and a rising standard of living in Member countries, while maintaining financial stability, and thus to contribute to the development of the world economy;
- to contribute to sound economic expansion in Member as well as non-member countries in the process of economic development; and
- to contribute to the expansion of world trade on a multilateral, non-discriminatory basis in accordance with international obligations.

The original Member countries of the OECD are Austria, Belgium, Canada, Denmark, France, Germany, Greece, Iceland, Ireland, Italy, Luxembourg, the Netherlands, Norway, Portugal, Spain, Sweden, Switzerland, Turkey, the United Kingdom and the United States. The following countries became Members subsequently through accession at the dates indicated hereafter: Japan (28th April 1964), Finland (28th January 1969), Australia (7th June 1971), New Zealand (29th May 1973), Mexico (18th May 1994), the Czech Republic (21st December 1995), Hungary (7th May 1996), Poland (22nd November 1996) and Korea (12th December 1996). The Commission of the European Communities takes part in the work of the OECD (Article 13 of the OECD Convention).

Publié en français sous le titre:
UNE NOUVELLE ÉCONOMIE ?
Transformation du rôle de l'innovation et des technologies de l'information dans la croissance

FOREWORD

This study examines the role of innovation and information and communications technologies in recent OECD growth performance. It is inspired by the strong economic performance of the US economy in recent years and is thus closely related to the debate on whether a "new economy" has emerged in the United States. The study was carried out in response to a mandate of the May 1999 OECD meeting at Ministerial level. It is not exhaustive, however, and several other aspects of the OECD work on growth are covered in other studies following on the Ministerial mandate. It is also a "work in progress", as further work on growth is to be carried out in preparation for the meeting at Ministerial level that will take place in 2001.

The study was prepared by an OECD team consisting of Alessandra Colecchia, Dominique Guellec, Dirk Pilat, Paul Schreyer and Andrew Wyckoff, with extensive input from Thomas Andersson, Daniel Malkin, Akira Masunaga and Risaburo Nezu. The analysis draws on various background documents, including a joint study with the OECD Economics Department and a recent study by Sam Paltridge on the pricing of Internet access. Statistical support was provided by Sandrine Kergroach-Connan. The study was carried out under the guidance of the Industry Committee, the Committee for Scientific and Technological Policy, and the Committee for Information, Computer and Communications Policy. Helpful input was obtained from forums dedicated to this subject organised in conjunction with the Industry Committee and the Committee for Scientific and Technological Policy. Participants at the meetings of these committees provided valuable comments. The study also benefited from comments within the OECD, in particular from colleagues in the Directorate for Science, Technology and Industry, the Economics Department, the Directorate for Education, Employment, Labour and Social Affairs, and the Directorate for Financial, Fiscal and Enterprise Affairs.

The study is published on the responsibility of the Secretary-General of the OECD.

TABLE OF CONTENTS

Executive summary 7

Introduction 17

Chapter 1. **Patterns of economic growth in OECD countries** 19

Chapter 2. **The changing role of innovation in growth performance** 27

Innovation and technological change have become more central to economic performance 27
Technology cycles have shortened 32
Market-based financing is now more important in funding innovation 32
 Financial systems are not equally effective in funding new firms 33
 Venture capital is important in supporting new technology-based firms and risky projects 34
A wider diversity of knowledge requirements implies a need for networks and openness 36
 Networks and alliances between firms are growing rapidly 38
 Foreign direct investment and trade links allow access to global knowledge 40
 Start-up firms play an important role in the innovation process 42
 Links to the science base are more important than in the past 42
 Knowledge-intensive business services are of growing importance for innovation 44
 Human capital is a key factor in innovation and skilled workers have become more mobile 44
The role of ICT in innovation 47

Chapter 3. **The role of information and communications technology in growth performance** 49

The aggregate evidence – significant investment in ICT and a rising contribution to growth 50
Evidence at industry and firm level 53
 The industry level: ICT increases productivity in using industries 53
 The firm level: ICT improves productivity by enabling organisational innovation 55
A new role for ICT in the 1990s? 56
Reaping the benefits from new ICT: are OECD economies on divergent paths? 62

Chapter 4. **Policies that support growth based on innovation and information technology** 73

Links between policy and economic performance 73
Policies to promote innovation and technological change 75
 Establishing a favourable climate for business 75
 New types of financing and improved risk management 76
 Funding for science and high-risk research 76
 Policies to strengthen co-operation and encourage diffusion 77
 Human capital to support innovation and technological change 78
 Enhancing the benefits of investment in ICT 78
Some final considerations 79

Notes 81

Bibliography 85

OECD 2000

The OECD growth project

Growth rates have diverged in OECD countries in the 1990s. At the same time, the United States has experienced very strong growth. The OECD Ministerial Communiqué of May 1999 requested the OECD to address variations in growth performance:

"*Growth performance* varies considerably across and within OECD countries. Ministers asked the OECD to study the causes of growth disparities, and identify factors and policies (such as rapid technological innovation and the growing impact of the knowledge society and its demand on human capital, the arrival of new service industries, the best framework conditions for fostering the start-up and growth of new enterprises including SMEs…) which could strengthen long-term growth performance."

Over the past year, the OECD has engaged in a range of studies to follow up on this mandate. An interim report is being delivered to the June 2000 meeting at Ministerial level. The work completed thus far has been partly of a fact-finding nature, *e.g.* analysis of trends and patterns in recent economic growth. Other aspects of the work have looked at some of the factors driving recent growth performance, *e.g.* the role of information technology and the role of innovation in services.

This report examines the role of investment in information and communications technologies (ICT) and innovation in recent growth performance in the OECD area and touches on some of the factors and policy areas of importance in moving towards a new economy. It is inspired by the strong economic performance of the US economy in recent years and relates closely to the debate on whether a "new economy" has emerged in the United States. It suggests that the relationship between technological progress, innovation and growth has changed in the 1990s and that certain OECD countries have proved better able to respond to and benefit from these changes than others. The report makes no attempt to be exhaustive. Other aspects of growth performance are treated in greater detail in other OECD work, such as that carried out by the Economics Department and the Directorate for Education, Employment, Labour and Social Affairs. A comprehensive analysis of all factors and policies affecting growth performance will be prepared for the meeting of the OECD Council at Ministerial level in 2001; it will also involve further analysis of factors and policies that determine innovation and investment in ICT.

EXECUTIVE SUMMARY

Patterns of economic growth in OECD countries

Analysis of growth patterns in the OECD area shows that levels of GDP per capita are no longer converging. In the 1990s, growth was higher in a few high-income countries, such as Australia, the Netherlands, Norway and the United States. In addition, countries such as Ireland and Korea continued to catch up to higher income levels. But growth in Japan and in much of continental Europe, notably its larger economies, was slower than in the 1980s, in some cases owing in part to macroeconomic shocks.

In the 1990s, levels of GDP per capita diverged across OECD Member countries.

The increasing divergence of labour utilisation rates provides one explanation for the increasing discrepancies in GDP per capita. Greater labour utilisation can make a significant contribution to growth over the short and medium term, as the experience of Australia, Ireland and the United States shows. Countries with higher per capita growth rates maintained or even increased employment over the 1990s, while employment stagnated or fell in those experiencing a slowdown in growth of GDP per capita. Labour productivity continued to converge in the 1990s (see Figure 3), in part as a result of labour shedding in countries with weak employment growth.

This disparity is largely due to the fact that some countries were able both to increase the number of people working and increase their productivity.

In some cases (*e.g.* Australia, Denmark, Ireland, Finland, Norway, the United States), labour productivity growth rates are linked to significant technological progress, as estimated by the growth of multi-factor productivity (MFP), which reflects the overall efficiency with which labour and capital are used. It is also affected by managerial practices, organisational change and, more generally, improved ways of producing goods and services. In many countries, MFP is a more important driver of labour productivity than greater availability of capital per worker. In the second half of the 1990s, MFP accelerated in Australia, Finland and Ireland, but also, and, in contrast to the early 1990s, in the United States. Recent data for the United States show an acceleration in MFP growth, with rates doubling from about 0.6% over the period 1991-95 to 1.25% over 1996-99.

Productivity (MFP) gains are largely the result of technological developments coupled with smarter ways of working.

An empirical analysis of growth patterns shows that no individual factor can be singled out as the main source of differences in growth performance. Several indicators, such as the pick-up in MFP growth in some countries, the growing importance of technological progress embodied in investment goods such as ICT, and the importance of skills, point to technology and innovation as important factors in recent growth performance.

Technology and innovation are key drivers of increased growth performance.

The changing role of innovation in growth performance

The relationship between science, technology and economic performance appears to have changed in the 1990s...

The relationship between technological progress, innovation and growth appears to have changed in the 1990s. The ways in which organisations interact in an economy have been affected, with networking, co-operation and the fluid flow of knowledge within and across national borders gaining in importance. Some countries in the OECD area have thus far been better able to respond and benefit from the change than others. The United States is of particular interest because it has made sizeable gains in MFP although it is already one of the most productive and technologically sophisticated countries.

...and innovation is now more critical to the success of firms and ultimately the growth of economies.

In this changing environment, innovation has become more market-driven, more rapid and intense, more closely linked to scientific progress, more widely spread throughout the economy. Services sector R&D, for example, rose from less than 5% of total business enterprise R&D for the OECD area as a whole in 1980 to more than 15% in 1995. In countries that measure services R&D well, such as Canada, it now amounts to about 30% of total business enterprise R&D.

ICT has played an important role in facilitating innovation.

In many cases, ICT, particularly since the recent emergence of the Internet, the World Wide Web, the browser and electronic commerce, has facilitated these changes by significantly reducing the costs of outsourcing and co-operation with entities outside the firm. It has helped break down the natural monopoly character of services such as telecommunications, it is a key technology for speeding up the innovation process and reducing cycle times, it has fostered greater networking in the economy, it makes possible faster diffusion of codified knowledge and ideas and it has played an important role in making science more efficient and linking it more closely to business.

In this changing environment, new ways to reduce costs in the search for new ideas are evolving.

Because the costs and risks of innovation have increased, firms have become more specialised, shifting from an inward to a more outward orientation. The role played by research in firms' commercial strategies has also changed. As the range of technologies required for innovation has expanded and technologies have become more complex, companies can no longer cover all relevant disciplines. Many key developments draw on a wide range of scientific and commercial knowledge, so that the need for co-operation among participants in different fields of expertise has become greater in order to reduce uncertainty, share costs and knowledge and bring innovative products and services to the market.

Networking and openness are of growing importance for innovation...

...for technological advances and the setting of standards...

Empirical studies suggest that collaboration is an important factor in the discovery, application and diffusion of technologies and may sometimes be motivated by a desire to develop *de facto* technological standards in the formative periods of new technologies. A notable example is the development of the GSM standard, which has facilitated extremely rapid growth in the use of mobile phones in Europe. Many co-operative agreements are linked to firms' difficulties in using and implementing ICT, and particularly to the need for compatibility and interoperability, for instance in banking and airlines. Available data show that the number of alliances has grown rapidly, particularly in areas such as information technology and biotechnology. The number of new intraregional ICT alliances, for example, rose threefold between the early 1980s and the mid-1990s. In 1998, strategic alliances were the source of a quarter of the earnings of the top 1 000 firms in the United States, double the share in the early 1990s.

Patenting also indicates the tendency of countries to seek sources of innovation and knowledge wherever they exist, and cross-border ownership of patents – where the applicant (owner) resides in a different country than the inventor – has increased considerably in the 1990s (see Figure 12). The internationalisation of patenting has not been equally rapid in all countries: the available evidence shows that US patents have a larger, and more rapidly growing, proportion of foreign co-inventors than those of Europe or Japan.

...as trends in patenting reveal.

Countries such as Australia and the United States have benefited substantially from the immigration of highly skilled personnel. There are indications that the United States was able to sustain rapid growth in the ICT sector, particularly in the software segment where human capital is the key input, by tapping into international sources of skilled workers. Immigration may therefore be one of the factors that have enabled the US boom to continue, as it filled some of the most urgent skill needs (see Figure 17).

Because human capital is a key factor in the innovation process, openness to ideas from abroad and efforts to attract or use skilled human resources abroad are increasing...

There is growing evidence that innovation in areas such as ICT or biotechnology draws increasingly and more directly on scientific progress. In the United States, the Bayh-Dole Act (1980), which extended patent protection to publicly funded research, helped to strengthen the role of science in the innovation process and was an early step in facilitating industry-university collaboration. Since then, further policy reform in this area has facilitated innovative performance. A recent analysis of US patent citations found, for example, that more than 70% of citations in biotechnology were to papers originating solely at public science institutions, while a study of scientific publications in the United Kingdom showed that the proportion of articles authored by industry scientists with an academic co-author rose from 20% in 1981 to 40% in 1991.

...as are industry-university links.

Start-up firms are important sources of new ideas and innovation and may have an advantage over larger established firms in emerging areas where demand patterns are unclear, risks are large, and the technology has yet to be worked out. Microsoft is a notable example of a firm that began life as a start-up. In the United States, large firms – Cisco is one example – "go shopping" in Silicon Valley and buy up or buy shares in small innovative projects. In 1999, Microsoft acquired shares in 44 firms (for USD 13 billion) and Intel in 35 (for USD 5 billion).

Start-ups are more flexible and unencumbered than large established firms and are essential to the "creative destruction" that occurs in periods of technological change.

However, they need the support of financial systems, including venture capital, which are capable of evaluating and monitoring high-risk innovative firms.

Start-ups require financial backing and often management help as well. At present, the United States has by far the most developed venture capital market. Internet-related investment represented over half of all US venture capital investment in 1999. In terms of level of investment in venture capital, Europe – where traditional banks play a major role – lags the United States. In Japan, venture capitalists, largely subsidiaries of banks, tend to invest small stakes in many firms, in order to diversify risk. In FY1998, the average size of a deal was USD 0.5 million in Japan, as compared to USD 4.7 million in the United States and USD 1.1 million in Europe. Where venture capitalists in the United States are often involved in the management of start-ups, this is frequently not the case in Europe or Japan. The share of venture capital investment in the early stages of the development of a project also remains relatively low in Europe and Japan.

In short, a broad set of factors creates the foundation that supports innovation-intensive economic growth.

Innovation and information technology are closely related in recent growth performance. Some recent changes in the innovation process and related impacts on innovation could not have occurred without ICT. Conversely, some of the impact of information technology might not have been felt in the absence of changes in the innovation system and the economy more broadly. Policies to encourage innovation and foster growth performance therefore need to address both areas.

The role of information and communications technology in growth performance

The rapid diffusion of ICT, so far most conspicuously in services, best exemplifies the shift in the relationship of innovation, science, technology and the economy.

Investment in ICT is making an important contribution to growth and labour productivity growth across the OECD. The 1990s witnessed rapid accumulation of ICT equipment. In the G7 countries (and most likely in other OECD countries as well) ICT investment progressed at two-digit figures over the past two decades and accounted for 10-20% of total non-residential investment in the business sector. However, while computers seem to be everywhere, use of ICT is actually concentrated in the services sector and a few manufacturing sectors. In constant (chained 1996) prices, US investment in information processing equipment and software as a share of total equipment and software increased from 29% in 1987 to 52% in 1999. The diffusion of ICT accelerated after 1995 as a new wave of ICT, based on applications such as the World Wide Web and the browser, spread rapidly throughout the economy. At relatively low cost, these technologies link the existing capital stock of computers and communications systems in an open network that significantly increases their utility.

ICT's contribution to output and labour productivity growth is rising…

The contribution of ICT capital to output and labour productivity growth has been significant and rising in relative terms. In Canada, the United Kingdom and the United States, ICT equipment contributed about half of fixed capital's contribution to output growth. The Bank of Korea reports that 40% of recent GDP growth in Korea came from the ICT sector, five times its 1999 share in GDP. In many cases, the measurable contribution of ICT to macroeconomic growth and MFP is still small, although sectoral and firm-level studies indicate a strong positive link between ICT use, productivity and output growth. Recent data for the United States show that about half of the pick up in MFP growth over the period 1996-99 occurs in industries other than ICT.

ICT is the technology area with the highest rate of innovation as measured by patents. Of the overall growth in patents granted by the US Patent and Trademark Office over 1992-99, ICT accounted for 31% and rose by almost 20% annually. The high rate of patenting points to the many changes in ICT hardware and software needed to use ICT effectively. More generally, ICT is enabling many changes in the economy and the innovation process that help make other economic sectors more innovative.

...along with its contribution to innovation, as increased patenting indicates.

The services sector is by far the main purchaser of ICT equipment and its performance has been particularly affected by the take-up of ICT. Services sectors such as finance and business services lead in investment in ICT and many services are now highly innovative. Moreover, services have become more tradable, with the result that they are more exposed to competition and are led to innovate to improve the quality of service offered and therefore remain or become competitive. Efforts to improve measurement of services output by introducing quality adjustments to capture the effects of improved service characteristics, such as easier and more convenient transactions and intermediation, typically result in upward revisions of these sectors' productivity. For instance, a study of the US banking industry shows output growing by over 7% a year between 1977 and 1994, instead of 1.3% according to the traditional measure.

Services play a leading role in the adoption of ICT.

The Internet and electronic commerce appear to be able to make a substantial contribution to economic growth, particularly in service industries. Here again, countries differ. The Nordic countries, Canada and the United States lead in terms of Internet host density. In September 1999, the host penetration rate for the United States was three times the average for the OECD area, seven times that of the European Union and just over eight times that of Japan. Between 1999 and March 2000, the United States added an additional 25.1 Internet hosts per 1 000 inhabitants, compared to an additional 5.5 Internet hosts for the United Kingdom, 4.1 for Japan, 3.0 for Germany and 2.7 for France. In short, instead of other countries catching up to the United States, the gap appears to be widening. Moreover, as of March 2000, the United States had six times as many secure servers per capita as the European Union, nine times more than France, eleven times more than Japan and sixteen times more than Italy. Even the Nordic countries, traditionally leaders in communication infrastructure, currently lag behind the OECD average. Here again, the most recent data show that the United States has been expanding its lead (see Figure 28).

The advent of the Internet and e-commerce has created a potential for further innovation...

The Internet has also been at the heart of a further deepening of ICT investment, by making possible a sharp increase in the quality and functionality of existing ICT equipment. It creates an

...largely thanks to low-cost, open access, which markedly lowers barriers for electronic commerce.

11

environment that substantially lowers the entry barriers for electronic commerce, in part because it adheres to non-proprietary standards based on the existing communications infrastructure. The low cost of connecting to the Internet and its independence from specific equipment or operating systems mitigates the opportunity costs of being locked in to a particular technology and reduces the "switching costs" that accompanied the adoption of earlier forms of e-commerce. In countries like Denmark and Finland that have attempted to measure e-commerce through the Internet, over half of firms with more than 20 employees used the Internet for ordering in 1999, up from about 15% in 1997, while 40% of firms received orders over the Internet, up from just 7% in 1997.

However, the Internet's most profound economic impact may in fact be its effect on existing industries that are adopting ICT and restructuring to exploit the new technology.

In agriculture, the Internet is providing better information about market prices and has fostered the emergence of new online commodity markets. In construction, it reduces the need for blueprints and allows seamless communications between subcontractors. In manufacturing, it is generating new efficiencies by reducing procurement costs and improving supply chain management. Its role in the services sector is linked to qualitative aspects of products, such as convenience and customisation, thereby reducing costs and delays and increasing reliability.

While technology diffusion and investment in ICT offer the potential for stronger growth, organisational change is indispensable.

ICT seems to offer the greatest benefits when ICT investment is combined with other organisational assets, such as new strategies, new business processes, new organisational structures and better worker skills. In a recent US survey, a quarter of all firms reported that they have made organisational changes to respond to the changes wrought by the Internet. For example, US durable goods manufacturers reduced inventories as a share of sales by more than a quarter between 1989 and 1999. This does not take into account savings associated with not having to finance inventories, warehouse them and discount them to accommodate shifts in demand.

Policies to support growth based on innovation and information and communications technology

To make effective use of the opportunities offered by ICT, countries need to ensure an environment conducive to innovation and receptive to new technologies.

A preliminary examination of the policies that help support innovation and investment in, and diffusion of, ICT suggests that a range of complementary factors and policies matter. Countries' ability to respond to rapid technological change greatly depends on the availability of the right set of skills and well-functioning product and capital markets. Collectively, these factors create an environment conducive to innovation and receptive to new technologies. The most recent evidence on the US economy points to the strong positive impact of ICT on economic growth and performance, probably enabled by the "right" environment.

Competition is a necessity.

Firms invest in innovation and in efficiency-enhancing technology if they can expect sufficient returns and if competition forces them to do so. Competition is also important for driving down the cost of technology. This is crucial for diffusing technologies such as ICT and the Internet throughout the economy. Technological change itself has resulted in the removal of the monopoly character of many parts of the telecommunications market and thus contributed to the introduction of greater competition and regulatory reform. Countries such as Australia, Denmark, the Netherlands and the United States have already undergone a long process of regulatory reform aimed at greater competition.

Investment in ICT is making an important contribution to growth and labour productivity growth across the OECD. However, OECD countries differ in their take-up of ICT, partly due to the varying pace of telecommunications market liberalisation. Where it is slow, this has limited investment in the necessary infrastructure and raised costs. Many successful OECD countries moved early to liberalise the telecommunications and information technology industries.

Liberalisation of telecommunications markets and regulatory reform facilitate investment in ICT...

There is evidence that the Internet and electronic commerce can make a substantial contribution to economic growth, particularly in service industries. But the take-up of the Internet differs considerably across OECD countries. The Nordic countries, the United States and Canada are the leading nations in terms of Internet host density. Regulatory frameworks, the pricing of local calls – including the taxes imposed – and a low critical mass of ICT users in some countries are among the important factors that contribute to cross-country differences in the diffusion of the Internet.

...since the price of telecommunications affects the diffusion of ICT and thus the Internet.

The ability to establish technology alliances between firms, to engage in mergers and acquisitions, and the degree of openness to trade and foreign direct investment all play a significant role in innovation as key developments in new areas draw on a wide range of scientific and commercial knowledge and make co-operation a necessity. However, co-operation in pre-competitive research needs to be balanced with a strong role for competition authorities at later stages. In addition, as OECD countries do not seem to look equally towards international sources of knowledge and technology, this may affect innovation and technological change.

The degree to which openness and collaboration are facilitated may help explain differences in innovation patterns and growth performance.

Links between science and industry are not equally developed across OECD countries. While reforms are under way, recent OECD work suggests that regulatory frameworks and deficient incentive structures continue to limit co-operation in many countries. Several successful countries, including Denmark, Finland and the United States seem to be characterised by strong links between science and industrial innovation.

Policies favourable to collaboration between science and industry are important...

Scientific institutions, including their links to the business sector, are important for technology diffusion and innovation. Science is also of increasing importance if countries want to benefit from the global stock of knowledge. Basic scientific research is the source of many technologies that are transforming society, such as the Internet and the laser, while research on the genome is contributing to advances in health care and biotechnology. Clearly government has an important role to play in the funding of scientific

...but public support for basic scientific research remains important to increase the stock of fundamental knowledge and to provide highly skilled graduates.

13

research, but there are likely to be diminishing returns to investment in science and governments will need to consider carefully the appropriate amount of public investment.

Furthermore, innovation in emerging areas requires favourable conditions for start-up firms.

Differences in the business environment for start-ups, such as their access to human capital and venture capital, the degree to which they are subject to administrative regulations, and the conditions for entrepreneurship, may affect innovation and economic performance. Many "successful" OECD economies, such as Australia, Denmark, Ireland and the United States, have relatively low administrative barriers for start-ups.

Differences in financial systems and the availability of venture capital also play a role.

Differences in financial systems, particularly the degree to which they are able to finance risky projects, may affect innovation in emerging industries and therefore growth, as new firms have limited access to finance and may be unable to grow or invest in innovation. Countries with well-developed financial markets and active venture capitalists may be better geared towards innovation and the reallocation of capital to such new industries than countries where traditional banking plays a dominant role.

The lack of a sufficient supply of skilled personnel is a key barrier to innovation and needs to be addressed.

Human capital is a key factor in the innovation process and many innovation surveys suggest a lack of skilled personnel as one of the crucial barriers to innovation. While a case can be made for greater international mobility of human resources, countries also need to address education, skills upgrading and human resource management at the domestic level. Initial levels of education are no longer sufficient in an economy in which demands change continuously; lifelong learning is increasingly important. Creativity, working in teams and cognitive skills are needed as economies become more based on innovation and technological change.

Attention needs to be given to ensuring access to new technologies and to providing people with the basic tools and skills for using them.

While innovation and technological change appear very important for strengthening growth performance, they may also have undesirable effects. There are concerns that the rapid spread of information technology may lead to a "digital divide" between those with access to the technology and those without. This may reinforce the skill bias of technological change and increase the gap in opportunities between low-skilled and high-skilled workers. In addition, some OECD countries have concerns that the financial benefits from innovation may accrue to only a small proportion of the population and increase earnings inequalities. It is unclear to what extent these effects are significant, as many are not new and recent US experience suggests a decline in income inequalities and higher employment rates for low-skilled workers. Rapid technological change has often been accompanied by major social changes and policy makers can help best by providing people with tools and skills that enable them to adjust to these changes, such as lifelong learning and well-functioning labour markets.

While countries may differ in their tendency to adapt to the new environment, policy changes can help ease the transition....

It has been argued that some countries and cultures may be better able than others to adapt to rapid growth and innovation. Cultural attitudes may affect people's willingness to take risks, to start a firm or to migrate. They may also affect a country's institutional framework. Cultural – and institutional – factors may therefore affect the transferability of policies and policy instruments and reduce the relevance of the US experience to other OECD countries. However, culture is not a static concept and attitudes towards risk and entrepreneurship may, for instance, be affected by changes in taxation, regulations, labour markets and the education system. Issues such as trust and basic confidence in society are also important in this respect and are the topic of ongoing OECD work.

It is essential to bear in mind that to use ICT and the Internet as a basis for innovation requires more than simply buying equipment or wiring schools. It is necessary to have the broader framework conditions that support organisational change, labour mobility, product market competition, training for new skills, a willingness to experiment and take risks and an openness to ideas, whatever the source.

...so that countries reap the benefits of economic growth through innovation which some have already achieved.

INTRODUCTION

In recent years, the US economy has grown at a surprisingly fast pace, in a phase of expansion that started nine years ago and constitutes its longest-ever recorded period of sustained growth. US GDP growth has exceeded that in the European Union in all but three of the last 20 years, and in Japan in all but three of the last ten years. As a result, US per capita income is now moving even further ahead of other OECD countries (Scarpetta *et al.*, 2000). Moreover, the expansion has been marked by low unemployment, record employment growth, low inflation and an acceleration of labour and multi-factor productivity (MFP) growth in the most recent years. Such strong growth performance is not uncommon amongst catching-up countries, but is unusual for a country that is already at the world productivity frontier in many areas. The long period of expansion coincides with high investment in, and diffusion of, information and communications technology (ICT) and its applications. The term "new economy" has been coined to mark the association of non-inflationary, sustained growth with high investment in ICT and restructuring of the economy (Box 1).

Box 1. The new economy: what do we mean by it?

The term "new economy" has been used extensively in recent years to describe the workings of the US economy and in particular the part of its economy that is linked to ICT. It reflects a view that something has changed and that the economy now works differently. Few studies clearly define the term "new economy" and it seems to mean different things to different people. The three main characteristics of the new economy appear to be the following:

The new economy may imply higher trend growth. Due to more efficient business practices linked to ICT use, the new economy may experience a pick-up in trend growth, due to higher MFP growth.

The new economy may affect the business cycle. ICT, in combination with globalisation, may change the short-run trade-off between inflation and unemployment and lower the NAIRU (non-accelerating inflation rate of unemployment). As a result, the economy can expand for a longer period without inflationary pressures emerging. In this view, ICT puts downward pressure on inflation, while increased global competition keeps wage inflation in check. More extreme views have argued that the new economy may mean the end of the business cycle.

The sources of growth are different in the new economy. Certain parts of the new economy may benefit from increasing returns to scale, network effects and externalities. The value of communications networks and Internet applications, for instance, increases as more people are connected. This situation entails considerable spillovers, and these contribute to higher MFP growth and fuel further growth.

These three characteristics are closely related and the US experience of the past decade provides some support for all, although there is no support for extreme claims about the end of the business cycle. It is not yet clear to what extent the US economy has indeed entered a new era, however, and concerns have been raised in recent years about macroeconomic imbalances and the way they will be unwound.

Source: Based on Stiroh (1999).

It is against the background of strong US performance that Ministers asked the OECD in 1999 to "study the causes of growth disparities, and identify factors and policies (such as rapid technological innovations and the growing impact of the knowledge society and its demand on human capital, the arrival of new service industries, the best framework conditions for fostering the start-up and growth of new enterprises including small and medium-sized enterprises – SMEs) which could strengthen long-term growth performance".

The present study responds by discussing recent growth performance in the OECD area and the role played by innovation and technological change, and information technology in particular. It focuses on these factors, since they are considered to be among the most important and because the Ministerial mandate specifically mentioned the role of innovation. The report is therefore not exhaustive; other important aspects of improvements in growth performance are addressed in greater detail in other OECD work. Consequently, the study is preliminary in nature. Its findings, and its policy implications in particular, will be further elaborated in the second year of the OECD work on economic growth.

To structure the analysis of economic growth and its causes, this document relies on a simple framework (Figure 1). It has three major features. First, as the left-hand part of Figure 1 indicates, it explores some of the "proximate" sources of growth. These relate to the familiar factors of production, labour and capital, and to their productivity. All changes in an economy's production can be attributed to changes in the quantity of labour or capital employed, to changes in the quality of these inputs or to advances in technology and efficiency (the productivity component). Chapter 1 discusses some findings that emerge from an examination of these proximate sources (Scarpetta *et al.*, 2000).

Second, the central part of Figure 1 evokes some of the underlying ("ultimate") determinants of growth. Many potential determinants exist and several are noted above. They include investment in fixed capital, human capital and innovation, the degree of an economy's interaction and openness, the strength of the diffusion process, mobility of human resources and cost factors. This study focuses primarily on the factors related to the role of innovation and technological change in growth performance (Chapter 2) and to information and communication technologies (Chapter 3). No claim is made that these are the only important drivers of growth, or that they alone constitute the most important ones. However, the report asserts that a number of recent changes in OECD economies primarily concern these areas.

Third, the right-hand part of Figure 1 is closely linked to the central part and concerns the impact of policy and institutional factors on these determinants of growth. It addresses the role of macroeconomic policy, product, financial and labour market policies, regulatory reform, technology and innovation policy, etc. As noted above, the policy implications of this document are preliminary in nature and will be explored further as analysis in other parts of the OECD is completed. Chapter 4 offers a number of initial policy conclusions.

Figure 1. **Analytical framework**

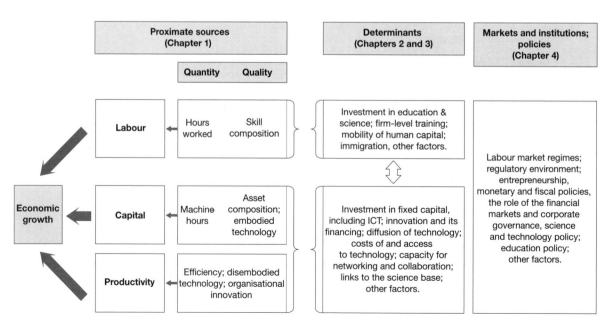

Source: OECD.

Chapter 1

PATTERNS OF ECONOMIC GROWTH IN OECD COUNTRIES

Before examining some of the proximate sources of growth, it is useful briefly to examine the main growth patterns in the OECD area. Much of this section is based on joint work with the OECD Economics Department, and supporting tables and further detail can be found elsewhere (Scarpetta *et al.*, 2000). In what follows, growth is measured as GDP and as GDP per capita, the most widely accepted indicators. It is well understood that these measures are not synonymous with welfare and not suited to catch all dimensions of economic growth, such as environmental or social concerns. However, consumption possibilities are an important aspect of welfare, and income growth usually raises sensitivity to environmental and social issues and the means allocated to deal with them.

Divergence in growth patterns. Although GDP growth continued to slow in most OECD countries in the 1990s, the trend reversed in some countries and was sustained to the end of the decade. Using GDP per capita as the measure of growth, a similar, but even more accentuated, picture appears (Figure 2). Countries' growth performances differed markedly. More specifically, the spread of GDP per capita growth rates increased between the 1980s and the 1990s. A good deal of this variation is due to greater divergence among countries of the European Union, where growth rates picked up in several smaller countries, notably Denmark, Ireland, the Netherlands and Norway, and slowed in France, Germany, Italy and Sweden. OECD-wide differences widened as well, with high and sustained growth in the United States and Australia and a sharp drop in activity in Japan. Special circumstances, such as German unification, and macroeconomic shocks in Finland, Korea and Japan, have contributed to slower growth in some countries. The acceleration in growth in Australia, Denmark, Ireland, the Netherlands, Norway and the United States is not a purely cyclical phenomenon. When a trend-cycle breakdown is carried out (Scarpetta *et al.*, 2000), it appears that the trend and actual growth rates of GDP per capita are broadly consistent.

Labour utilisation and labour productivity. Growth in GDP per capita can be broken down into GDP per hour worked and total number of hours worked in relation to the population. The first component, GDP per hour worked (Table 1), measures aggregate growth of labour productivity; the second is a measure of labour utilisation. Thus, growth rates in GDP per capita will diverge if differences between countries' labour productivity gains increase and/or if labour utilisation rates diverge. Over time, rates of labour utilisation have tended to diverge across OECD countries, and this provides one explanation for the increasing discrepancies in GDP per capita. Greater labour utilisation can make an important contribution to growth in the short and medium term; it has substantially benefited growth in Australia, Ireland and the United States in the 1990s (Figure 3). Though not unlimited, the potential for faster growth from higher levels of labour utilisation is far from exhausted, especially in continental Europe where employment rates are low, especially among youths, prime-age women and older workers. Moreover, policy may affect migration flows. This is especially important, as the population in most OECD countries is ageing, and the working age population is likely to decline unless it is supported by migration flows.

Catch-up by some countries. Whether or not countries grow rapidly, a large part of growth in per capita income is due to changes in labour productivity. In many countries where output growth per capita accelerated, it was due to the a combined effect of higher labour productivity and greater labour utilisation. Several of the fastest-growing countries in the 1990s also had positive gains in labour utilisation, in particular Korea, Ireland, the Netherlands, Norway and the United States. In the debate about differences in countries'

Figure 2. **Growth performance in the 1980s and 1990s**

Average annual rates of change of GDP per capita

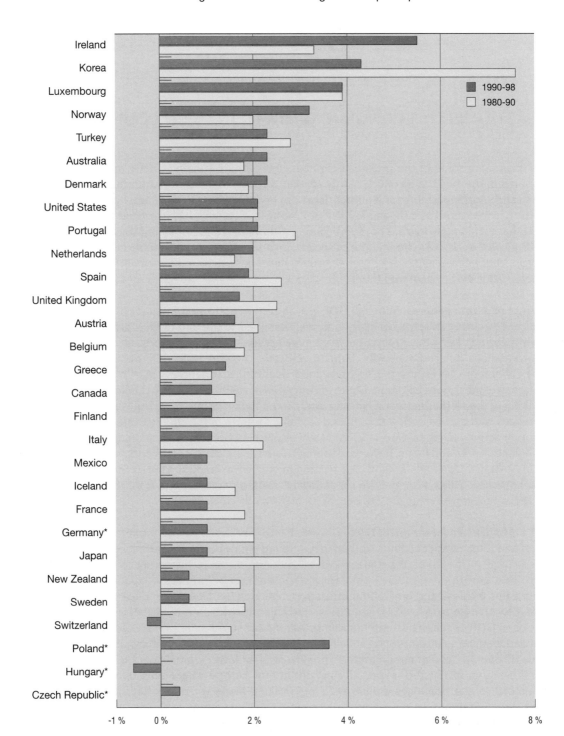

* Data for the Czech Republic, Germany, Hungary and Poland start in 1991. Germany before 1991 is Western Germany.
Source: Scarpetta *et al.* (2000), based on *OECD Economic Outlook* No. 66.

Table 1. **Growth and productivity in the business sector**

Percentage changes at annual rates

	Output (business sector GDP)			Employment (number of persons)			Hours per person			Output per employed person			Output per hour		
	1980-90	1990-95	1995-98[4]	1980-90	1990-95	1995-98[4]	1980-90	1990-95	1995-98[4]	1980-90	1990-95	1995-98[4]	1980-90	1990-95	1995-98[4]
United States	3.2	2.5	4.5	2.0	1.3	2.4	-0.1	0.2	-0.1	1.2	1.2	2.1	1.3	1.0	2.2
Japan	4.1	1.5	1.1	1.3	0.6	0.3	-0.4	-1.5	-0.8	2.8	0.9	0.9	3.3	2.4	1.6
Germany[1]	2.4	1.6	1.8	0.5	-0.8	-0.2	-0.7	0.1	0.0	1.9	2.4	1.9	2.6	2.2	1.9
France	2.4	1.0	2.5	0.0	-0.7	0.8	-0.8	-0.5	-0.2	2.5	1.6	1.6	3.3	2.1	1.9
Italy	2.3	1.4	1.4	0.4	-1.1	0.4	-0.3	-0.5	0.3	1.9	2.5	1.1	2.2	3.0	0.8
United Kingdom	3.2	2.6	3.0	0.7	0.8	1.7	-0.5	-0.2	-0.3	2.5	1.9	1.3	3.0	2.1	1.6
Canada	2.8	1.8	3.3	1.6	0.4	2.4	-0.1	-0.1	-0.2	1.2	1.4	0.9	1.3	1.5	1.1
Australia	3.6	3.3	4.8	2.4	1.2	1.6	0.0	0.1	-0.3	1.2	2.2	3.2	1.3	2.1	3.5
Austria	2.3	1.9	3.0	-0.1	0.4	0.2	-	-	-3.4	2.4	1.5	2.8	-	-	6.2
Belgium	2.0	1.5	2.5	0.1	-0.2	1.3	-	-0.7	-0.1	2.0	1.7	1.2	-	2.4	1.3
Switzerland	2.1	-0.2	1.5	1.6	-1.0	0.3	-	0.1	-1.2	0.5	0.8	1.2	-	0.7	2.3
Czech Republic[2]	-	4.3	0.5	-	1.0	-0.8	-	-	0.1	-	3.3	1.3	-	-	1.2
Denmark	1.9	3.0	3.2	0.3	-0.7	2.0	-	0.1	0.6	1.7	3.7	1.2	-	3.6	0.6
Spain	2.7	1.3	3.5	0.1	-1.4	2.7	-0.9	-0.1	0.1	2.6	2.7	0.8	3.5	2.8	0.7
Finland	3.0	-0.5	5.8	-0.1	-4.7	2.4	-0.5	0.1	-0.3	3.1	4.3	3.3	3.6	4.1	3.6
Greece	1.3	1.4	3.3	0.7	0.6	0.7	-	0.1	0.1	0.6	0.8	2.6	-	0.7	2.5
Hungary[3]	-	0.2	3.8	-	-5.9	0.5	-	1.2	0.4	-	6.1	3.2	-	4.9	2.8
Ireland	4.3	4.9	9.7	-0.1	2.0	6.7	-	-0.9	-0.7	4.5	2.9	3.0	-	3.9	3.7
Iceland	-	0.5	5.5	1.3	-0.5	2.2	-	-0.1	-0.3	-	1.0	3.3	-	1.1	3.6
Korea	9.4	7.5	1.9	2.9	2.3	-0.9	-0.7	-0.2	-1.3	6.5	5.2	2.8	7.2	5.5	4.1
Luxembourg	-	5.3	4.9	-	2.4	3.3	-	-0.5	-0.6	-	2.9	1.7	-	3.5	2.3
Mexico	-	0.9	5.6	-	2.7	3.7	-	0.3	0.8	-	-1.7	2.0	-	-2.1	1.2
Netherlands	2.2	2.2	3.7	0.6	0.8	3.0	-1.7	-1.5	0.5	1.6	1.4	0.7	3.3	2.9	0.2
Norway	1.0	2.4	4.2	-0.1	-0.3	2.8	-	-0.3	-0.3	1.1	2.8	1.4	-	3.0	1.7
New Zealand	1.8	3.3	1.8	0.4	3.0	1.2	-	0.3	-0.3	1.5	0.3	0.6	-	0.0	0.9
Poland[3]	-	5.5	6.7	-	-2.0	1.3	-	-0.2	-0.3	-	7.5	5.4	-	7.7	5.7
Portugal	2.7	1.5	3.8	1.1	-2.2	1.5	-	-0.6	-1.7	1.6	3.7	2.2	-	4.3	3.9
Sweden	2.3	1.0	2.4	0.6	-2.1	0.4	0.3	0.8	0.2	1.7	3.2	2.1	1.5	2.3	1.9
Turkey	5.3	3.2	5.7	1.3	2.0	2.0	-	-	-	4.1	1.3	3.8	-	-	-

1. 1980-90: Western Germany; total Germany as of 1991.
2. Data start in 1993.
3. Data start in 1991.
4. 1998: provisional data.
Source: OECD Economic Outlook No. 66; Scarpetta et al. (2000).

labour productivity growth, the "catch-up" hypothesis is frequently evoked. It suggests that countries with initially low income levels should grow faster in subsequent years, because they are able to catch up with the leading countries. The underlying idea is that less advanced countries are in a position to benefit from other countries' technology, know-how and experience and so raise their labour productivity growth at a comparatively rapid rate.

Empirical examination shows that the catch-up hypothesis contributes to the growth dynamics of some, but by no means all, countries. Higher than average growth rates in GDP per capita in Ireland, Korea, Poland and Portugal are indeed consistent with their relatively lower levels of GDP per capita at the beginning of the 1990s (Scarpetta et al., 2000). Along the same lines, Switzerland's slow output growth per capita seems to fit above-average initial income levels. However, this is not universally a factor for explaining growth. Most prominently, the United States' expansion accelerated over an extended period, despite being the country with the highest income per capita and one of the highest levels of output per hour worked. Similarly, for Denmark, the Netherlands and Norway, the catch-up hypothesis provides few insights, so that the drivers of strong growth have to be sought elsewhere. Moreover, some countries, such as Mexico, had comparatively low per capita income and labour productivity but did not catch up.

Figure 3.   **The role of labour utilisation and labour productivity in growth**
Total economy, 1990-98

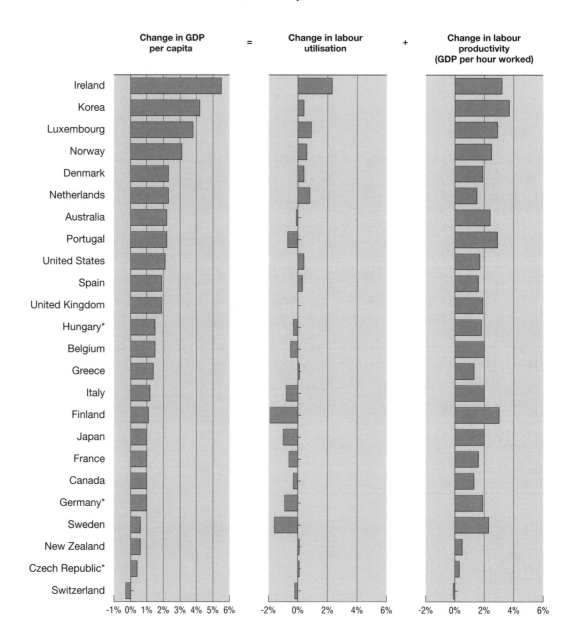

* Data for the Czech Republic, Germany and Hungary start in 1991. Germany before 1991 is Western Germany.
Source: Based on *OECD Economic Outlook* No. 66, and Scarpetta *et al.* (2000).

Considerable differences in GDP per capita persist in the OECD area. While a good deal of catch-up has taken place, there is still considerable diversity in levels of GDP per capita in the OECD area (Figure 4). The United States leads in income distribution, followed by Norway and Switzerland, with GDP per capita at 80-90% of the US level. Most other OECD countries, including all other major economies, have income levels at 65-75% of the US level. A number of lower-income economies follow, including Greece, Korea, New Zealand, Portugal and Spain, some of which have experienced very high growth over the recent period. Mexico, Turkey and two of the former centrally planned economies (Hungary and Poland) fall at the bottom of the OECD income distribution.

Figure 4. **Levels of GDP per capita and labour productivity**
United States = 100

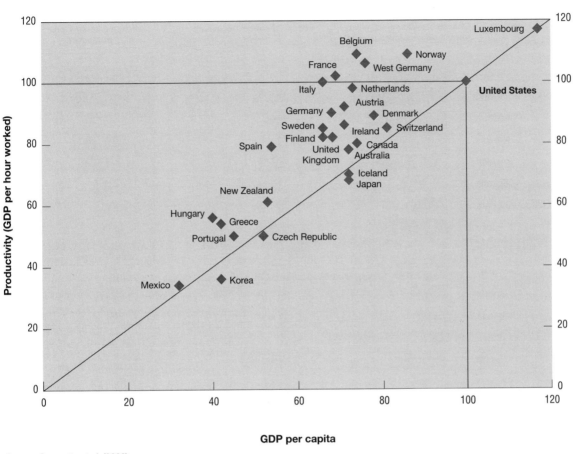

GDP per capita

Source: Scarpetta *et al.* (2000).

The US lead in labour productivity is less pronounced, and some countries have labour productivity levels above that of the United States (Figure 4). This seems linked to low levels of labour utilisation, as labour productivity gains in these countries largely reflect shedding of low-skilled workers and the substitution of capital for labour (Scarpetta *et al.*, 2000).

Capital deepening and overall productivity. Rising labour productivity itself depends on the rate of capital deepening, *i.e.* the services provided by capital equipment to each worker, and on multi-factor productivity. The faster capital deepening occurs, the more rapid the growth of labour productivity, *i.e.* output per worker. The overall evidence suggests that capital deepening plays an important, but not a dominant role in explaining increased labour productivity over the 1990-95 period (Figure 5). This does not imply, however, that investment has been unimportant to the process of growth. For instance, if growth in output is driven both by investment and employment, the capital-labour ratio may remain constant or change little. In addition, capital deepening may primarily have occurred in some areas of capital equipment, thereby

Figure 5. **The role of capital deepening and MFP in growth, 1990-95**
Business sector

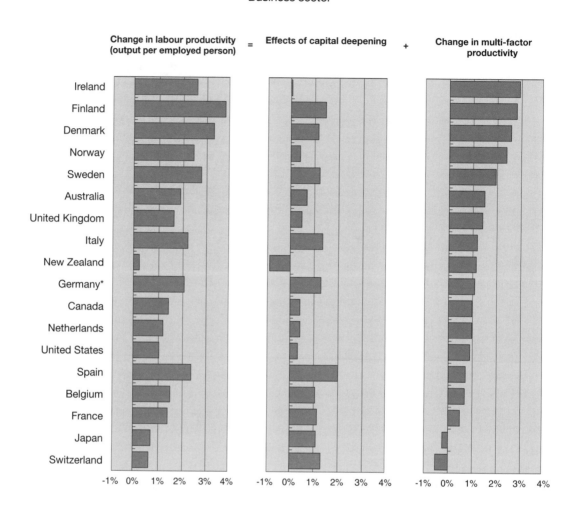

Change in labour productivity (output per employed person) = Effects of capital deepening + Change in multi-factor productivity

* Data for Germany start in 1991.
Source: Based on *OECD Economic Outlook* No. 66, and Scarpetta *et al.* (2000).

affecting the composition of the capital stock. While the evidence is somewhat limited, it appears that ICT constitutes a singularly dynamic component of business investment in capital equipment. Across G7 countries (and most likely in other OECD countries as well), ICT investment progressed by double-digit figures over the past two decades, accounting for 10-20% of total non-residential investment in the business sector.[1] Investment in ICT is discussed further in Chapter 3.

Productivity picked up in several countries. Multi-factor productivity reflects the overall efficiency with which labour and capital are used. It is affected by a host of factors, including innovation, technological change and its diffusion, managerial practices, organisational change and, more generally, improved ways of producing goods and services. In many countries, MFP is a more important driver of labour productivity than capital deepening (Figure 5). In the second half of the 1990s, MFP accelerated in Australia, Finland and Ireland, but also, and in contrast to the early 1990s, in Japan and the United States (Figure 6). The United States' pick-up in labour productivity and MFP has been remarkable in that it occurred at a comparatively late stage of the business cycle. It has been taken as a key element of the "new economy", as it enabled the expansion to continue while keeping inflation low.

Figure 6. **The role of capital deepening and MFP in growth, 1995-97**

Business sector

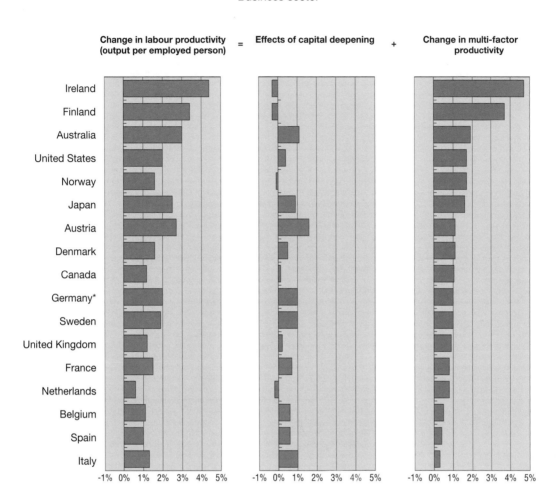

* Data for Germany start in 1991.
Source: Based on *OECD Economic Outlook* No. 66, and Scarpetta *et al.* (2000).

Chapter 2

THE CHANGING ROLE OF INNOVATION IN GROWTH PERFORMANCE

Chapter 1 pointed to various factors driving differences in growth performance across the OECD area. Economic growth can be achieved through increased or improved use of labour and capital or through a rise in multi-factor productivity (MFP). None of these factors stands out as being the single most important in all OECD countries. In some countries where growth has accelerated in recent years (notably Australia, Denmark, Finland, Ireland, Norway, the United States), however, growth has been accompanied by above-average increases in MFP. Growth in MFP can arise from several sources, but among the most important are "disembodied" technological change (*e.g.* organisational change and learning by doing) and spillovers from investment in innovation and knowledge. In addition, a significant part of technological change is "embodied" in capital equipment; the growing role of information and communication technologies (ICT), in particular, points to quality improvements in capital equipment. Finally, OECD analysis provides evidence that employment growth has been skill-biased and that quality changes in labour input play an important role in recent growth trends (Scarpetta *et al.*, 2000).

This suggests that innovation and technological change are indeed important factors in recent growth performance. While others, notably improved labour market performance, also play a significant role, this study focuses primarily on innovation and technological change, which are arguably among the most important "new" elements of recent growth. Other factors are addressed in other parts of the OECD work on growth (*e.g.* Scarpetta *et al.*, 2000). Developments in ICT are clearly the most important source of technological progress in the 1990s, but changes in innovation and the innovation process go beyond ICT. Some changes in the innovation process, such as the greater role of networking, are closely linked to ICT. Conversely, some of the impacts of ICT would probably not have occurred without broader changes in the innovation system. This section examines the role of innovation in recent growth performance in the OECD area and analyses some of the main factors determining the degree of innovation and technological change in OECD countries. Chapter 3 focuses on the role of ICT.

Innovation and technological change have become more central to economic performance

Innovation and technological change are commonly considered as being among the most important drivers of economic growth.[2] However, it is difficult to capture their contribution in empirical analysis. A variety of approaches, at firm, sector and economy-wide level, have been used to link them to economic growth (OECD, 2000a). They show that innovation and technological change are indeed important determinants of economic growth, but that their precise contribution is difficult to assess and quantify (Box 2).

Although the evidence is incomplete, various indications point to the growing importance of innovation and technological change in economic performance. First, investment in innovation is rising. OECD expenditure on research and development (R&D), though only part of total investment in innovation, was almost USD 500 billion in 1997, or more than 2.2% of OECD-wide GDP, following a strong surge in spending in the second half of the 1990s. While the overall R&D intensity of OECD economies has not regained its peak of 1989-90, the composition and funding of R&D has changed significantly. Civilian R&D has gained in importance relative to defence-related R&D, and business R&D to government-funded R&D. The decline in defence research, following the end of the cold war, may have helped stimulate innovation, particularly in the United States, as much defence research is very specialised, with few civilian applications, and the confidentiality of defence research does not favour diffusion of its results.

Box 2. **The empirical links between technological change, innovation and growth**

The literature on innovation, technological change and growth provides evidence for a number of stylised empirical links. These are based on the empirical application of economic theory, including neo-classical theory, "new" growth theory and evolutionary theory (OECD, 2000a). The main empirical links are:

R&D provides an important contribution to output and total factor productivity growth. The empirical evidence typically show that a 1% increase in the stock of R&D leads to a rise in output of 0.05-0.15%. There is also evidence that R&D may play a different role in small and large economies (Griffith *et al.*, 1998). In large countries, R&D mainly helps to increase the rate of innovation; in smaller ones, it primarily serves to facilitate technology transfer from abroad.

The private rate of return to investment in R&D is quite high, often 10-20%. Owing to technology spillovers, social rates of return to R&D investment are substantially higher (Cameron, 1998). It is therefore not only the invention of new products and processes and their initial commercial exploitation that generate major economic benefits, but also – and often rather – their diffusion and use. These spillover effects have an important global dimension. For many small OECD economies, knowledge and technology from abroad have a larger impact on productivity than domestically developed technology, although domestic investment in science and innovation is crucial to enable the absorption of such technology and knowledge transfers from abroad. The evidence also shows that there are considerable differences in rates of return across sectors, with R&D in research-intensive sectors having higher returns. In addition, basic research has higher rates of return than applied R&D, and process R&D often has higher returns than product R&D (Cameron, 1998).

There is a close relationship between investment in technology at firm level and productivity performance (OECD, 2000b). The relationship also exists at sectoral level, although it is weaker, given the wide variations in firm behaviour. At the economy-wide level, it is often difficult to establish a clear link between an indicator of technology effort and productivity growth. The difficulty has a number of sources (OECD, 1998a). First, both innovative effort and productivity may be incorrectly measured. Second, there may be a lag between innovative effort and its translation into productivity gains. Third, it is difficult to disentangle the impact of technology from other factors affecting productivity. Finally, a large part of economy-wide productivity gains are due to the diffusion process. The firm-level evidence shows that technological change can bring significant productivity gains, but only when accompanied by organisational change, training and upgrading of skills, *i.e.* when the new technologies are thoroughly "learned".

These links are not the only ones to be found in the empirical literature, but they are the best established and are supported by a large volume of literature. This is mainly because data on R&D are well-established, exist for many countries and over a long time period. Yet, the evidence goes beyond these three main links. First, differences in per capita income across countries are partly due to technology gaps (Fagerberg, 1994). This suggests that low-income economies may have a potential for catching up with high-income economies by applying technologies developed abroad. Second, useful evidence can be gathered from innovation surveys. They demonstrate that firms invest in innovation because they want to gain market share, reduce cost and increase profits. Innovation surveys covering 12 European countries suggest that over 30% of manufacturing turnover is derived from new or improved products (Department of Trade and Industry, 1999). Some empirical research based on these surveys confirms the role of innovation in improving firm performance (OECD, 2000a). Third, technology and innovation have important indirect impacts on economic performance. For instance, technological change has removed the monopoly character of many parts of the telecommunications market, enabling regulatory reform and the introduction of greater competition (Blondal and Pilat, 1997). This has led to improvements in this sector's productivity and a decline in costs, thereby facilitating the development of ICT goods and services, including electronic commerce.

Over the past years, R&D has thus become more market-oriented, and overall business funding of R&D has grown in many OECD countries, including the United States. Growth in business-funded R&D has been particularly rapid in a number of small OECD economies, such as Australia, Denmark, Finland, Iceland, Ireland, Korea and Sweden, where R&D intensity has risen significantly (Figure 7). In many OECD countries, business funding has gained in importance in overall R&D expenditure. Countries with large increases in the intensity of business R&D to GDP and in the share of business R&D in total R&D, including Australia, Denmark, Finland, Ireland and Sweden, appear to have experienced a pick-up in MFP growth in the 1990s (Bassanini *et al.*, 2000).[3] Increased spending on knowledge and innovation goes considerably beyond spending on R&D, however, and includes spending on education and software. Most OECD countries have also increased spending in these areas, and investment in these intangible assets is now as large as investment in fixed capital equipment (OECD, 1999a).[4]

Figure 7. **Trends in the intensity of business-funded R&D relative to GDP**

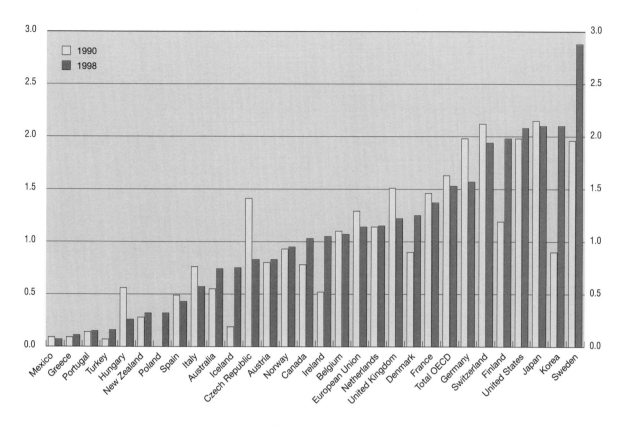

Source: OECD, MSTI database, November 1999; OECD (1999a).

Second, a surge in patenting, an indicator of the output of the innovation process, bears witness to the growing importance of innovation and helps to indicate the effectiveness of greater investment in innovation.[5] Data on numbers of patents granted in the United States indicate that the ratio of patents to GDP has increased considerably in most OECD countries over recent years (Figure 8).[6] This is even more clearly illustrated by US patent performance. Since the mid-1980s, the number of patents granted by the US Patent and Trademark Office (USPTO) to US and foreign inventors has risen steadily (Figure 9), close to the rates observed in the 1950s and 1960s (when GDP growth was substantially higher). Since 1995, patenting has grown exponentially (Council of Economic Advisors, 2000).

The European Patent Office has witnessed a similar surge in patenting, although it started later. The rapid growth is partly explained by changes in legislation (*e.g.* software is now patentable in the United States), but the evidence suggests that it is mostly due to rapid innovation across all technology fields (Kortum and Lerner, 1998a). Rapid innovation in ICT and biotechnology appears to account for the bulk of the increase. Of the overall growth in patents granted by the USPTO over 1992-99, ICT accounted for 31% and biotechnology for 14%. ICT patents rose by almost 20% annually over the 1992-99 period, and biotechnology patents by almost 9% annually (USPTO, 2000). This indicates that technological innovation has accelerated since the mid-1980s and suggests that economic growth is now more strongly linked to innovation.

Third, the innovation process appears to be spread more widely across sectors, as the services sector takes an increasingly important role in R&D expenditure (Figure 10). Services sectors such as finance and business services lead in investment in ICT (see below), and innovation surveys indicate that many services are highly innovative.[7] There is also evidence that, for services sectors such as banking, transport and

Figure 8.   **Patents granted in the United States**
Per billion USD of GDP, 1990 and 1998

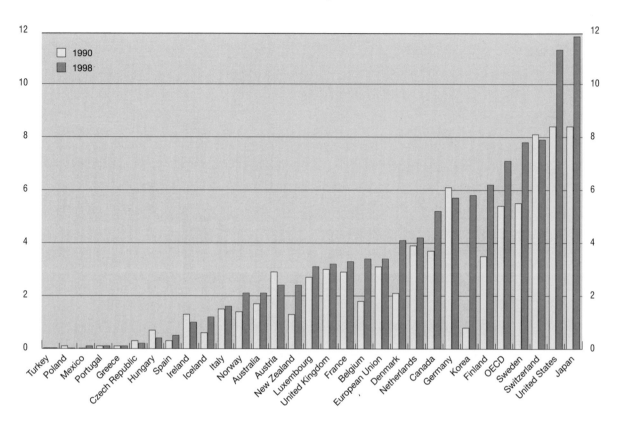

Source: Patents from US Patent and Trademark Office; GDP in PPP USD from Scarpetta *et al.* (2000).

Figure 9.   **Patents granted in the United States, 1990-98**
Annual number granted; compound annual growth rate over each period

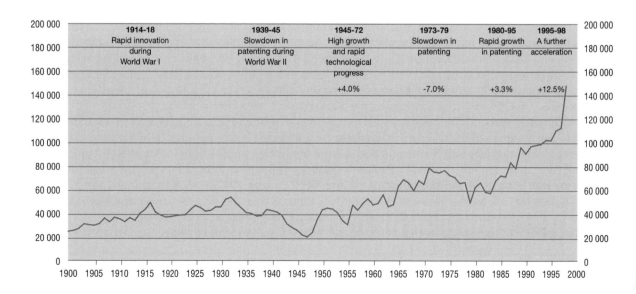

Source: US Patent and Trademark Office.

Figure 10. **Business expenditure on R&D in services**

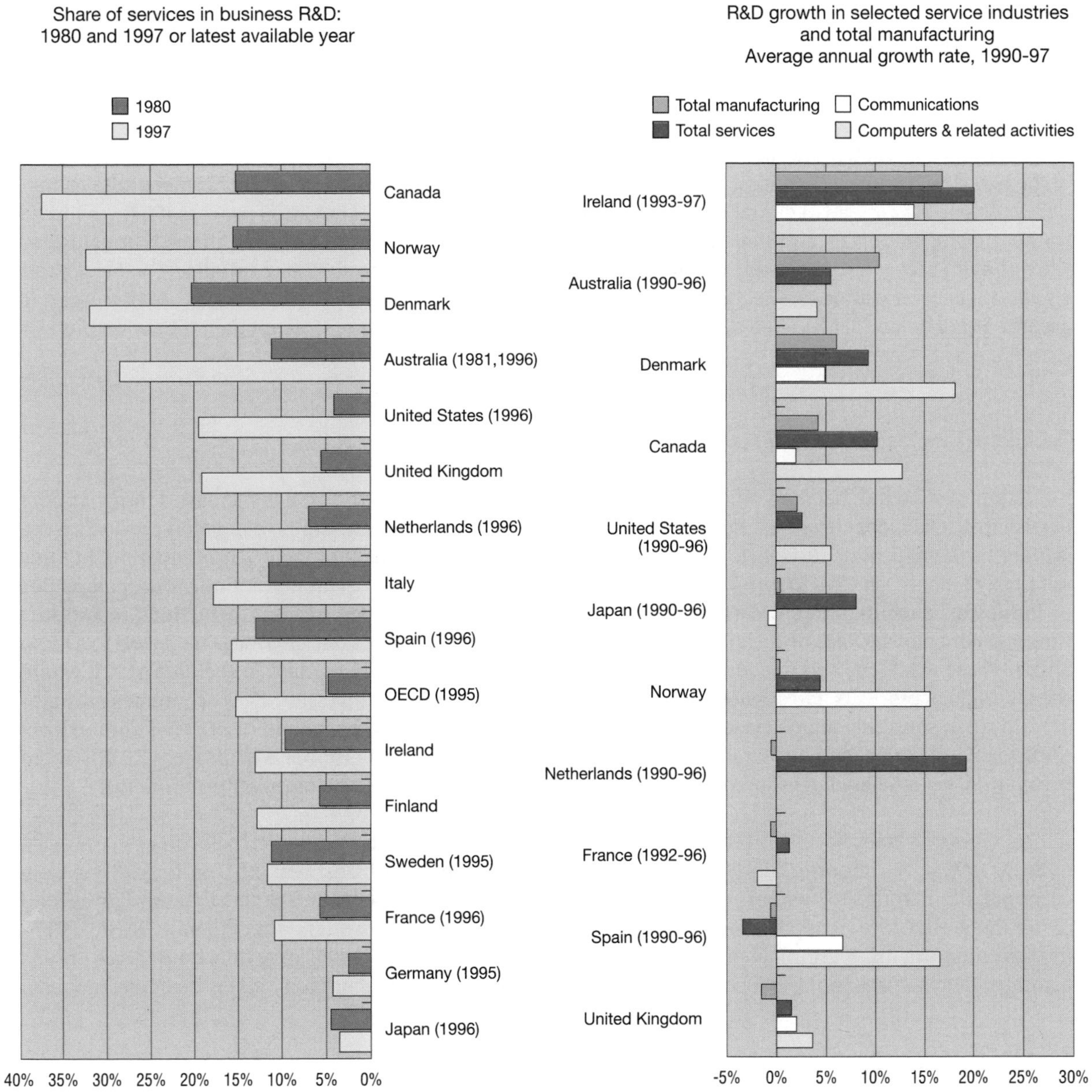

Share of services in business R&D: 1980 and 1997 or latest available year

■ 1980
□ 1997

R&D growth in selected service industries and total manufacturing
Average annual growth rate, 1990-97

□ Total manufacturing   □ Communications
■ Total services   □ Computers & related activities

Source: OECD, ANBERD database, May 1999.

retailing, ICT investment has enabled product and process innovation which has led to higher productivity growth (OECD, 2000b). Innovation surveys suggest that, on average, services are somewhat less likely to innovate than manufacturing, but that certain services, such as knowledge-intensive business services, are more likely to innovate than the average manufacturing firm (OECD, 2000b). Innovation surveys also indicate that many of the objectives of innovation in services are similar to those of manufacturing firms: increasing market share, improving service quality and expanding the product or service range.

Fourth, several indicators reflect the increasing impact of innovation and technological change on recent growth performance. Empirical studies suggest that firms' stock market valuations are closely linked to expenditure on R&D and other intangible assets, including links to top scientists or the Internet (Hall, 1999; Darby *et al.*, 1999. Desmet *et al.*, 2000). Scientific activity, as a key source of basic knowledge for innovation, continues to increase across the OECD area and has a growing and more direct impact on innovation (see below). In addition, technology flows play an increasing role in the balance of payments of OECD countries, and a growing share of exports originates from medium- to high-technology industries (OECD, 1999a).

This suggests that, more than before, innovation is now at the core of economic activity. In all sectors of the economy, including services, firms must innovate to respond to sophisticated consumer and business demands and stay ahead of global competition. Several changes in the innovation process itself are linked to the growing importance of innovation and technological change. There are indications that countries which have successfully adapted to these changes have been better able to capitalise on the greater significance of innovation and technological change in the growth process. These changes are discussed in greater detail below. ICT has had a major impact on many of them and therefore on the innovation process (see the end of Chapter 2).

Technology cycles have shortened

As innovation has become more important to business and competition has increased, firms appear to wish to obtain more concrete results from their R&D expenditure and pressures to develop products more rapidly have increased. Surveys for the United States suggest that the average R&D project time in firms fell from 18 months in 1993 to ten months in 1998 (NIST, 1999). Anecdotal evidence for individual companies in industries such as aircraft, cars, computers and machinery suggests similar reductions in product development times (Office of Technology Assessment, 1995). These reductions appear to be linked to a more applied research focus and to shorter product cycles. This is particularly evident in the area of ICT, where the life cycle of products and services has shortened most. Structural changes in OECD economies may also contribute to shorter research cycles. The composition of the business sector and of R&D has shifted from traditional industries (steel, chemicals) with long product cycles and an emphasis on process R&D to more innovative, faster-changing industries, often with short product cycles (*e.g.* computer equipment).

As research cycles have shortened, research has also become more closely tied to business strategies (OECD, 1998a). An important indicator of this change is the move of business R&D in large firms from corporate laboratories to business units. There is some evidence for the United States that this has helped companies translate research more effectively into successful products (Iansiti and West, 1997). Improvements in firm performance in the United States since the early 1990s may thus be due not only to a greater innovation effort, but also to much improved integration of technology in the business process.

Market-based financing is now more important in funding innovation

Finance is a key requirement for innovation. As the nature of innovation has changed, so have methods of financing it. Growth disparities may be partly related to OECD countries' uneven achievements in adapting to these changes. Certain financial systems that performed well in funding mature industries have been less effective in providing capital to emerging industries and firms. New firms tend to have little access to retained earnings (cash flow and depreciation); if this limits their access to finance, they may not be able grow or invest in innovation. A financial system that can address this problem is clearly an advantage in an economy where new industries, such as those based on information technology and biotechnology, are of growing importance.

Innovation raises special issues for finance, partly because it often demands a broader set of conditions, including entrepreneurship and human capital. Innovation is often risky and subject to considerable monitoring problems. Investors have difficulty appropriating some of the returns and may therefore be reluctant to finance innovative activities and innovative firms. This is particularly a problem for small firms and start-up companies, which may lack collateral and reputation, as well as sufficient market power to capture the rewards from innovation. Two issues are of particular importance in this respect:

- The role of financial systems, including secondary stock markets, in funding new firms, and the impact of cross-country differences in corporate governance systems.

- The emergence of venture capital markets, which combine the financing, management and nurturing of risky projects.

Financial systems are not equally effective in funding new firms

Following the financial liberalisation which began in the mid-1980s, financial systems have changed considerably in the OECD area, although the pace of change differs widely across countries. Financial markets (shares and corporate bonds) have gained in importance at the expense of bank credit, and companies rely increasingly on equity markets for capital. There are marked differences among countries, however, as regards the respective roles of banks and financial markets, the ownership and control of firms, financial regulations and corporate law. All countries have a mix of institutional and market-based financing, but some are predominantly bank-based, while in others financial markets are more important. In countries such as Germany and Japan, relations between firms and banks are close and ownership is highly concentrated. This type of corporate governance is typically referred to as an "insider system". Conversely, "outsider systems", found in countries such as the United States and the United Kingdom, are characterised by dispersed ownership and a stronger role for financial markets, both in providing capital and in determining business strategies.

The growing importance of innovation and the emergence of certain new industries has implications for the effectiveness of these systems. First, to finance new industries, the financial system needs to facilitate the process of creative destruction. This implies reallocating capital to new firms and new activities at the expense of declining ones. It also often involves changing firm boundaries through mergers, acquisitions and split-ups. Such a system differs from one primarily geared towards the accumulation of physical assets in large, stable firms in well-established industries, which were the basis for much economic growth in the post-war period.

The conditions for creative destruction may therefore be better guaranteed in "outsider" systems, where greater transparency and information disclosure and dispersed ownership are accompanied by relatively high flexibility. Changes in corporate control through mergers, take-overs or split-ups are also more common in systems with a large role for financial markets, as shareholders seek more systematically to maximise the value of the firm, than in bank-based systems. Mergers and acquisitions are far more common in the United States and the United Kingdom than in continental Europe or in Japan. Moreover, as they are a channel for industrial organisation and for the circulation of knowledge, technology may circulate more easily in countries with high M&A activity.[8]

Financial markets are also more transparent and able to write off the value of firms that perform poorly, hence releasing capital for new ventures. Most companies in the S&P500 (a US stock market index) experienced declining share prices or only small gains in 1999, although the index itself surged. Due to incurred sunk costs, banks are often more reluctant to write off loans and sell equity even when they know that its value has dropped. The process of "creative destruction", which is at the heart of the high-technology sector, may thus be better handled by financial markets than by banks and other financial institutions.

Insider systems also have some advantages, however. Concentrated ownership, as in Germany and Japan, tends to ensure more effective monitoring of management and may help to overcome agency problems between firms' owners and managers. Stable firms that are protected from take-overs may also have advantages. In mature industries, technological change is often more incremental, uncertainty is lower and learning is often linked to the accumulation of tacit knowledge over time. Bank-based systems may support long-term investment in such mature industries quite effectively (Maher and Andersson, 1999; Carlin and Mayer, 1999). Financial markets are often weaker in this area, where investment could become sunk in a specific economic activity (Bebchuk, 1999).

Treatment of risk is the major challenge in funding new firms and industries. The profitability of new ventures is uncertain; risky investments may result in high rewards in case of success but large losses in case of failure. As they lack collateral, and as future profits are potentially high but very uncertain, new firms may not be in a position to attract bank loans. In countries where banks have a major role in finance, governments have sometimes provided direct loans or bank guarantees to small and new firms. Such efforts cannot possibly address the financial needs of the entire economy and are not an alternative to well-functioning financial markets. In countries with underdeveloped financial markets, large established firms in existing industries have tended to be major players in new industries, as in the case of mobile telephony in Europe and Japan.

New firms generally rely on equity capital, which – depending on the maturity of the stock market – may be more readily available. Well-functioning equity markets may be more amenable to risky investment such as R&D than bank-based systems (Carlin and Mayer, 1999). While banks can often provide some measure of equity capital, financial markets have the advantage of allowing for competing views. Where there is uncertainty or a contradictory assessment of a project by investors, it will be easier to find funds on the stock market, where many investors operate, than in a limited number of banks.

For new firms, the high cost of access is a traditional disadvantage of financial markets. Firms need to gain investors' confidence and build reputation, respect strict rules of transparency and present strong past records. To address this problem, secondary financial markets have been set up in many countries (NASDAQ in 1973, various "new markets" in Europe since 1996, Japan in 2000). These are characterised by easier rules of access, especially as regards past records. Secondary markets have been very successful, judging by the number of firms quoted and the amount of capital raised. They are not always sufficient for risky projects, however. Venture capital fills this need, as it offers a way for business projects to mature in the earliest stages.

Venture capital is important in supporting new technology-based firms and risky projects

In the 1990s in the United States, venture capital (VC) investment played a key role in the funding of innovative firms; it is now developing rapidly in Europe and Asia. It is a major factor in the development of technology start-ups, as it is primarily aimed at the commercial implementation of a major innovative idea or technology. Venture capital consists of equity or equity-linked investments in young, privately held companies. The investor is a financial intermediary, which typically takes a role as director, advisor or even manager of the firm. VC investment goes considerably beyond financing, as it adds complementary measures to increase the chances of success. First, business plans are intensively scrutinised – a very low proportion of submitted plans are actually financed. Second, VC disburses funds by stages. To ensure that money is not wasted, managers of VC-backed firms must return regularly to their investors for additional capital. Third, VC monitors managers intensively, by demanding representation on the board of directors and preferential stock embodying restrictive clauses. In most cases, VC firms provide start-up firms with experienced management and strategic advice and give them access to a business network. Fourth, VC firms aim at integrating the technologies they handle to make them complementary. VC is thus much more than investment; it nurtures new firms in a process which is highly dependent on the venture capitalist's experience. These arrangements also help to mitigate the selection and monitoring process, often a key challenge for VC investors, owing to the complexity of technology, uncertainty with regards to future demand and the absence of a track record for the would-be entrepreneur.

While there are few systematic empirical studies, there is considerable evidence to suggest that VC investment has significantly influenced innovation and growth. Most large high-technology firms in recent decades are offspring of VC (*e.g.* Microsoft, Netscape, Compaq, Sun Microsystems, Intel, Apple, Digital

Equipment Corp., Genentech). Over the past 25 years, almost 3 000 US companies financed by venture capital have gone public. In 1999, 271 venture-backed companies went public in the United States, accounting for half of all initial public offerings (IPOs) (Thomson Financial Securities Data, 2000). When exploring the experience of 20 US industries over a 30-year period, Kortum and Lerner (1998b) found that VC-supported firms accounted for less than 3% of R&D investment, but for 15% of patenting in the 1990s. In addition, patents from VC-supported firms are more often cited and more aggressively litigated than other patents, an indication of their higher technological and economic value. VC-backed firms are also frequent litigators of trade secrets, a sign that they are also strong in non-patented technology.

VC investment is particularly important for emerging industries, and the bulk has been directed towards two areas, ICT and biotechnology. However, VC is only one component of the financial system, and will only be effective if the entire system works well. The possibility for investors to exit through an IPO is especially important, as investors engage their funds only if they can recoup their liquidity afterwards. Secondary financial markets, such as NASDAQ, EASDAQ, *Neuer Markt*, *Nouveau Marché*, are crucial in this respect as they allow the quotation of firms with limited track records.

As the VC industry is not yet equally developed across the OECD area, this may play a role in divergent economic performance. VC was traditionally a US industry, with some diffusion in Canada and to a lesser extent the United Kingdom. Since 1995, it has expanded rapidly in most European countries, although less in Japan. In the United States, VC experienced a rapid expansion in the early 1980s, when pension funds were allowed to invest part of their assets in risky ventures. A strong acceleration in the second half of the 1990s continued through 1999 (more than 100% growth for the first nine months of 1998). The recent surge in VC investment is fuelled mainly by Internet-related investment, which represented over half of all US venture capital investment in 1999 (OECD, 2000c).

Until a few years ago, the VC industry was small in Europe, with the exception of the United Kingdom and the Netherlands, and did not focus on high-technology segments and early-stage funding. It has surged in all countries since 1995 (at the same pace as in the United States), especially in technology-related fields. Belgium, Finland, France and Germany have experienced particularly high growth over the past four years. There is evidence of an emerging community of venture capitalists in all these countries. This will allow further development of VC. The share of early stages and expansion is still relatively low, however (Figure 11). In terms of level of investment in VC, Europe lags the United States by about two years. The share of foreign (non-European) capital in VC has jumped from about one-tenth in 1995 to one-third in 1998. Banks play a major role in funding VC in Europe, ahead of pension funds, the major source in the United States. Corporations contribute much less to VC funds in Europe than in the United States.

In Japan, as compared with other OECD countries, VC is still underdeveloped. Japanese venture capital firms provide financing mainly in the form of loans to established SMEs. Most funds ("VC associations") are affiliates of stockbrokers that make money more by underwriting the floatation than from their investment. Interest represents almost half of venture capital firms' income, and almost two-thirds of the funded firms were established more than ten years previously, compared to fewer than 20% in the United States. Japanese VC tends to invest small stakes in many firms, in order to diversify risk. In FY1998, the average size of a deal was USD 0.5 million in Japan, as compared to USD 4.7 million in the United States and USD 1.1 million in Europe. In FY1998, less than 2% of investment was for the creation of new firms, and more than 35% went to firms aged 20 years or more. VC funds in Japan are typically not involved in the management of firms and therefore do not bring any expertise to them. A key problem is the shortage of experienced venture capitalists that can not only assess the risks of proposed projects but also monitor the company and intervene if necessary. Since most of Japan's venture capital companies (165 in all as of March 1997) are subsidiaries of financial institutions, venture capitalists often are not very experienced. However, there are now some 50 independent venture capital companies, and the share of early-stage involvement has been increasing.

The data on VC investment shown in Figure 11 may overstate the importance of VC in different countries. The preceding discussion shows that it is not the size of VC investment alone that matters for its impact

35

Figure 11. **Venture capital investment in early stages and expansion as a percentage of GDP**

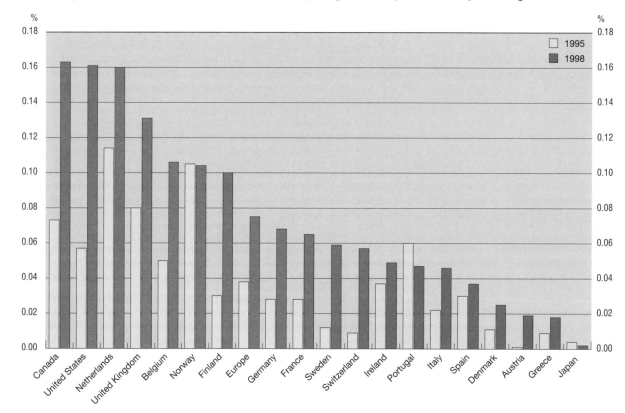

Source: European Private Equity and Venture Capital Association (EVCA) 1999 Yearbook; National Venture Capital Association (NVCA), 1999 Venture Capital Yearbook; Ministry of Trade and Industry Japan.

on the economy. Of equal importance is the quality of the support provided by venture capital firms to innovators. Other significant factors include the composition of investment, such as the share of investment channelled to early stages or high-technology firms; the number of deals being concluded; and the availability of complementary factors, such as the experience of venture capitalists. Anecdotal evidence suggests that the VC market is currently expanding very rapidly in the OECD area, particularly in Europe, and that a lack of VC capital is a less severe constraint than it was only two years ago.

Venture capital is often complemented by stock options which allow new, cash-less firms to hire, retain and motivate highly skilled staff whom they could not otherwise afford. Stock options imply that executives and employees are taking on a considerable amount of individual risk.[9] According to a survey by the National Venture Capital Association, 92% of venture-backed firms in the United States awarded stock options to their employees in 1996. While they were initially mainly provided to high level senior staff, an increasing number of companies, small and large, give options to a large proportion of their employees, and sometimes to all. In the United States, stock options have become so important that they are estimated to have reduced compensation growth by one-quarter of a percentage point a year between 1994 and 1998 (Lebow *et al.*, 1999). The use of stock options is expanding in other countries, if only to avoid a large gap in compensation with the United States.

A wider diversity of knowledge requirements implies a need for networks and openness

Increased competition, linked to globalisation and regulatory reform, appears to have had a substantial impact on the role played by research in firms' commercial strategy. In many firms, an important aspect of this change is a shift from an inward to a more outward orientation. With greater competition and globalisation, there is a wider variety of sources for new technologies and innovative concepts, many of them outside the direct control of firms. The range of technologies required for innovation has also expanded as innovation has moved closer to the scientific frontier and technologies have become more complex (Rycroft and Kash, 1999). Companies can no longer cover all main disciplines, as IBM and AT&T were able to do in the 1970s.

Monitoring other companies throughout the world and in different markets has therefore become an essential part of firms' innovative effort. In addition, as the costs and risks of innovation have increased, firms must increasingly co-operate with other firms to share the cost of bringing innovative products and services to the market and to reduce uncertainty.[10] Patent data show that a growing part of such co-operation takes place at international level (Figure 12). Cross-border ownership of patents – the applicant (owner) resides in a different country than the inventor – has increased considerably in the 1990s. In addition, for a growing share of patents, the co-inventors reside in different countries. The internationalisation of patenting has not been equally rapid in all countries; the available evidence shows that US patents have a larger, and more rapidly growing, proportion of foreign co-inventors than Europe or Japan.

Because large firms no longer "make" all their innovation in house in corporate laboratories, they have become more specialised in their core competencies and increasingly "buy" and co-operate in order to acquire complementary knowledge and technology. They gain access to the knowledge they require through several channels. Innovation surveys show that these include co-operation with other firms, *e.g.* through networks, alliances and joint ventures; purchase of capital equipment; involvement of specialist knowledge-intensive services; interaction with scientific institutions; integration of other firms and start-ups through mergers and acquisitions; and mobility of high-skilled human resources (Table 2). Such channels may be domestic or global.

The importance of several of these channels of knowledge transfer has increased over the past decade. Although the empirical evidence is limited, the following trends can be observed:

- The number of strategic alliances between firms has increased. Several address R&D and technology collaboration.

Figure 12. **Global trends in the internationalisation of technology**

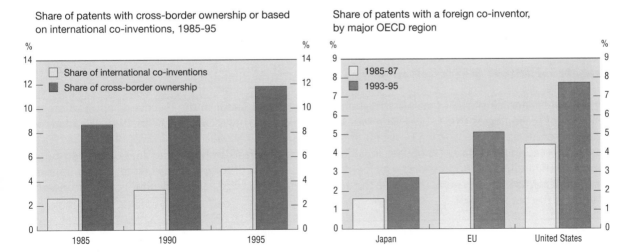

Share of patents with cross-border ownership or based on international co-inventions, 1985-95

Share of patents with a foreign co-inventor, by major OECD region

Source: OECD. Data are based on patent applications to the European Patent Office, by date of priority.

Table 2. **Relative importance of technology transfer channels**[1]

	Australia	Belgium	Denmark	France	Germany	Ireland	Italy[2]	Luxem-bourg	Norway	United Kingdom
Use of others' inventions	4	4	3	2	5	2	5	4	2	2
Contracting out of R&D	8	5	6	5	6	3	6	5	5	6
Use of consultant services	5	3	4	4	3	5	3	5	3	4
Purchases of other enterprises	7	7	7	7	7	6	8	8	6	7
Purchases of equipment	1	6	2	3	4	4	1	3	8	5
Communication services from other enterprises	2	2	1	1	1	1	2	1	1	1
Hiring of skilled personnel	3	1	5	6	2	7	4	2	4	3
Other	6	8	8	..	8	8	7	7	7	8

1. Importance was ranked from 1 (highest) to 8 (lowest). The table does not allow for direct comparison, as countries' response rates differ considerably.
2. Adjusted according to ISTAT. "Other" includes "purchase of projects".
Source: OECD (1999b).

- Trade and foreign direct investment continue to gain in importance. Trade in goods is growing most rapidly in high-technology industries. A rising part of FDI consists of mergers and acquisitions, which are partly driven by the need to gain access to knowledge. Trade in services is growing rapidly, diffusing new ideas and concepts.

- Links to the science base have become more important for innovation: industry patents make greater reference to public science and the business sector finances a growing share of research in universities and public laboratories.

- Knowledge-intensive business services, such as computer, R&D and training services, are among the economy's most rapidly growing sectors and play an important role in the innovation system.

- Human capital mobility has increased, including across national borders.

In combination, these patterns point to greater interaction within the economy and to the growing importance of collaboration. Not all countries have been equally successful in adapting to the need for greater openness and collaboration, however, and this may help explain differences in innovation patterns and growth performance.

Networks and alliances between firms are growing rapidly

Empirical studies suggest that collaboration is an important factor in the discovery, application and diffusion of technologies (NIST, 1998; Brouwer and Kleinknecht, 1999; OECD, 1999b). There is abundant evidence of increasing networking between firms, both in the same or different lines of business. Even non-collaborating firms do not innovate in isolation; they purchase embodied technologies, consultant services and intellectual property and scan for ideas from a variety of sources. Networking is also important for small firms, as it offers a way to combine the advantages of small size, such as flexibility, with economies of scale at the network level.

Networking can take many forms: research joint ventures, research contracts or cross-licensing agreements. Technology alliances and related co-operative arrangements allow firms to share costs, extend product range, and access new knowledge and markets. In 1998, one-quarter of the earnings of the top

Figure 13. **New international and intra-regional strategic technology alliances**

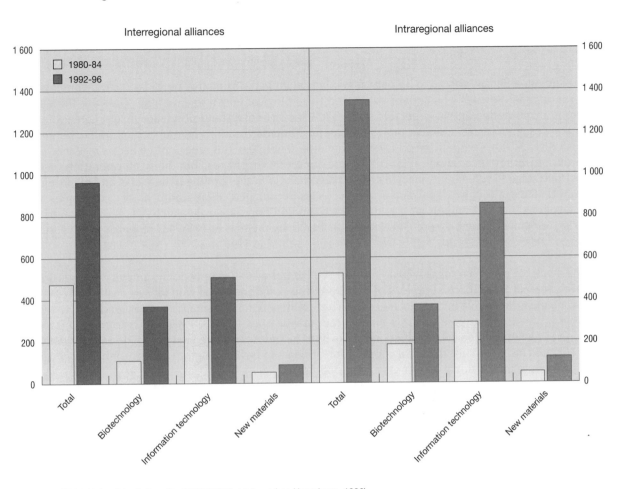

Source: NSF (1998a), originally from the MERIT-CATI database (see Hagedoorn, 1996).

1 000 firms in the United States were the result of strategic alliances, double the share in the early 1990s (Larson, 1999). Available data show that the number of alliances has grown rapidly in the 1980s and 1990s, particularly in areas such as information technology and biotechnology (Figure 13),[11] and that these have taken place both between major regions, such as the United States, Europe and Japan, and within them (NSF, 1998a).

Firms engage in these co-operative arrangements for several reasons.[12] First, the cost of major innovations, such as a new generation of semiconductors or aircraft, has risen rapidly and is now beyond the means of any single firm. Second, co-operation may enable the development of *de facto* technological standards. Particularly in services, many co-operative arrangements aim to establish such standards, as these may permit compatibility between different technologies and reduce technological uncertainty. Many of these co-operative agreements are linked to firms' difficulties in using and implementing ICT, and particularly to the need for compatibility and interoperability, for instance in banking and airlines (NIST, 1998).[13] It may in fact be crucial to develop a common standard in order to guarantee a sufficiently large market. For example, the development of the GSM standard has provided a strong impetus to the development of mobile telephony in Europe, and to the current leadership of Nokia and Ericsson in this market (McKelvey, forthcoming). Indeed, for innovation in many areas, establishing a large market may be crucial, since it may be the only way to recover high development costs. Third, because many key

39

technological developments, including biotechnology, are complex, they draw on a wide range of scientific and commercial knowledge. This reinforces the need for the co-operation of participants in different fields of expertise (Rycroft and Kash, 1999). Fourth, highly skilled researchers are scarce in several important areas, and firms may find it useful to share them. Finally, joint ventures may reduce duplication of research and thus improve its efficiency.

Technology alliances appear to be particularly important in the formative periods of new technologies, when no dominant design or standard exists and technological uncertainty is high. They are therefore prevalent in knowledge-intensive sectors such as ICT, biotechnology and pharmaceuticals. Later, when a dominant design emerges and economies of scale and standardisation develop, co-operative ventures diminish (Pyka, 2000). Competition policy plays an important role in this area; it often allows research joint ventures and other technology alliances in pre-competitive phases, but bans co-operation at the competitive stage. Government policy has also played a role in the forming of networks and alliances. In the United States, a series of legal changes in the 1980s encouraged collaboration among companies and sectors. Among the most important was the 1984 National Cooperative Research Act, which allowed US firms to co-operate on generic, pre-competitive research. By the end of 1996, 665 research joint ventures had been registered under this Act, of which almost one-third in 1995 and 1996 (NSF, 1998a).[14]

The available evidence suggests that inter-firm collaboration still mainly occurs among domestic firms. However, foreign firms, both suppliers of materials and components as well as key customers, play a significant and growing role in national innovation networks, and firms in small countries tend to have more technology alliances with foreign firms than with domestic ones (OECD, 1999a). According to a Danish survey, internationalisation of innovation networks does not necessarily weaken domestic linkages (OECD, 1999b). In fact, increased international competition appears to have strengthened Danish networks while opening them to international customers and suppliers.

While international co-operation is of growing importance, local co-operation continues to be significant, as the success of Silicon Valley shows. The strength of local clusters is commonly associated with the value of tacit knowledge for the innovation process and with the localised nature of knowledge spillovers. Tacit knowledge, such as that embodied in skilled personnel, is less easily acquired at a broader level, as face-to-face contact and proximity count. In addition, clusters often rely on local advantages, such as concentrations of highly specialised skills and knowledge, institutions, rivals, related businesses and sophisticated consumers (Porter, 1998; OECD, 1999c). For instance, a recent study of Japan and the United States suggested that adoption of biotechnology by industrial firms is often closely linked to competencies of the local academic science base (Darby and Zucker, 1999). It can be argued that these local advantages will be the main source of future comparative advantage, since they are not readily mobile. Many countries' efforts to build clusters and centres of excellence seem partly based on this view.

Foreign direct investment and trade links allow access to global knowledge

Trade and FDI remain significant sources of innovative ideas and concepts and may take on greater importance as the complexity of innovation at technological frontiers makes it increasing difficult for individual firms and countries to engage in innovative activities. High-technology industries have experienced the greatest increase in international trade during the 1990s (Figure 14), much of which is intra-industry trade and reflects the splitting of production and innovation processes across the globe to take advantage of local knowledge and comparative advantages. Growing trade and global competition in these high-technology industries have created scale economies, which have put downward pressures on prices (Mann, 1999).

The increase in high-technology trade is not spread equally across the OECD area. By the late 1990s, the three main regions of the OECD – the European Union, Japan, the United States – all had roughly the same trade exposure as a share of GDP, about 8-10% (OECD, 1999a). The United States' exposure increased gradually over the 1990s, however, while that of Europe – excluding intra-European trade – increased more

Figure 14. **Growth of OECD manufacturing trade by industry and technology intensity[1]**
Average annual growth rate, 1990-96

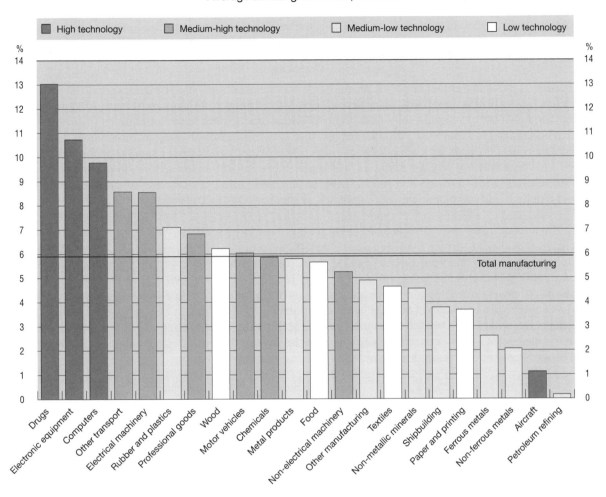

1. OECD excludes the Czech Republic, Hungary, Korea, Mexico and Poland. Average value of exports and imports.
Source: OECD, Main Industrial Indicators database, 1999.

slowly. Japan's trade exposure is the lowest and most unbalanced and has changed little since 1993. Further work is needed to determine the exact contribution of trade to productivity growth, but the literature clearly shows that trade embodies efficiencies and promotes competition that improves productivity. Preliminary evidence suggests that an increase in exposure to international trade, such as that experienced by the United States, may have a larger impact on productivity than high but stable exposure to trade (Mann, 1997).

In recent years, trade also increasingly affects sectors of the economy previously considered non-tradable, thereby strengthening competition and the diffusion of new concepts, technologies and ideas to these (services) sectors, and contributing to improved performance. In several services, such as retailing and retail banking, expansion at international level is important once firms face saturated domestic markets. It also allows companies to gain access to new knowledge, innovative concepts, services and ideas, and to new technologies.

Foreign direct investment has grown more rapidly than trade over the past decade. It plays a particularly large role in diffusing knowledge and ideas in services sectors, where local presence is often a necessity.   41

Its relative importance varies markedly across countries. Countries with a large net inflow of FDI, such as Ireland, are likely to obtain important net benefits from technology and knowledge flows. Countries like Japan, where the stock of inward investment remains very small relative to GDP, are less likely to benefit from technology and knowledge inflows. Outward FDI is undertaken for many purposes, such as gaining access to markets and benefiting from local research capabilities and knowledge spillovers. While market access has always been important, particularly in services, it has become more so.

Recent studies suggest that domestic productivity benefits if outward investment goes to R&D-intensive countries, an indication that FDI is aimed at obtaining ideas from abroad (Lichtenberg and Van Pottelsberghe, 2000). To benefit fully from such spillovers and exploit local capabilities, however, firms need to undertake their own R&D. The data suggest that, with the exception of Japan, the seven largest R&D-performing countries have seen a considerable rise in the percentage of R&D financed by foreign sources since 1981. In addition, foreign affiliates are much more important in sectors like computers and pharmaceuticals (about 60% and 50%, respectively, of 1997 production) than for low- or medium-technology sectors like food and motor vehicles (20% and 30%, respectively) (OECD, 1999d).

In the area of trade and FDI, there are several other new factors in the 1990s. First, the nature of FDI has changed markedly, with mergers and acquisitions now accounting for more than 85% of total FDI (Kang and Johansson, 2000). Over the 1991-99 period, cross-border M&A grew more than tenfold. As markets become more global and the cost of innovation – and production more generally – increases, economies of scale have become more important; in many industries the optimal size of firms seems to have increased.[15] This has contributed to a wave of M&A, which represented USD 3.4 trillion in 1999, after USD 2.5 trillion in 1998, already a record year. In contrast to past M&A, most now aim at reinforcing the core business of firms. The ten largest M&A in 1999 were all between firms in the same industry (Kang and Johansson, 2000). While technology is only one factor in the rise in M&A, it is a far from trivial one.

Start-up firms play an important role in the innovation process

Small start-up firms have gained prominence in the innovation process, as they are important sources of new ideas and innovations. In emerging areas, where demand patterns are unclear, risks are large, and the technology has not been worked out, small firms have an advantage over large established firms. They can be more flexible, are more specialised and may also be better at channelling creativity and providing the right incentives than large firms.[16] New mechanisms, such as venture capital and the associated entrepreneurial expertise, have allowed these firms to grow rapidly.

A small share of all start-ups either grow rapidly (e.g. Microsoft) or are purchased by large firms which then develop and commercialise their technology. In the United States, it has become part of the technology strategy of large firms (e.g. Cisco) to go shopping in Silicon Valley after the market has first screened innovative projects. For instance, Microsoft acquired shares in 44 firms for USD 13 billion in 1999 and Intel in 35 firms for USD 5 billion. Large firms such as Cisco, Intel and Microsoft also provide venture capital to start-ups. The changing innovation process has brought small start-up firms to the fore, as they are exploring new frontiers (electronic commerce, genetic engineering) and developing specialised niche markets. The United States' experience contrasts somewhat with that of Europe. Many European Internet companies are spin-offs of existing (telecommunications) enterprises. This may partly be linked to different conditions for start-ups in Europe and the United States (Nicoletti et al., 1999), but may also reflect a need in Europe to develop more flexible structures outside the control of existing firms, as existing firms may be too rigid.

Links to the science base are more important than in the past

To feed the innovation process, the business sector relies on scientific research and interaction with the science system.[17] Basic scientific research is the source of many of the technologies that are transforming society, including the Internet. Innovation in key sectors such as information technology and biotechnology, in particular, is closely linked to advances in basic science. The science system provides other economic benefits, however (Salter and Martin, 1999). Apart from its role in increasing the stock of fundamental knowledge, publicly funded research provides the skilled graduates that are essential to firms wishing to adopt new technologies, new instruments and methods for industrial research and an increased capacity for scientific and technological problem-solving. Scientific institutions also play a role in the formation of the world's research and innovation networks, which are increasingly considered crucial to technology diffusion and innovation. Thus, countries will need a sufficiently developed scientific infrastructure if they want to benefit from the global stock of knowledge. Finally, science plays a role in creating new firms or spin-offs (OECD, 2000d).

The science system's influence on innovation is now more direct. Available evidence suggests that interaction between the science system and the business sector is more prominent than in the past (Figure 15) and that in many fields technological innovation makes more intensive use of scientific knowledge. A study of scientific publications in the United Kingdom showed that the proportion of articles authored by industry scientists with an academic co-author rose from 20% in 1981 to 40% in 1991 (Hicks and Katz, 1997). Similar trends are present in the United States (NSF, 1998a). A recent study (Narin *et al.*, 1997) revealed that 73% of references to published articles in patents were to "public" science – university, government and other public institutions. The number of references to public science nearly tripled over the six-year period covered.

The links between science and industry are very strong in areas such as pharmaceuticals, organic and food chemistry, biotechnology and semiconductors but weaker in areas such as civil engineering, machine tools and transport (OECD, 1999b). In ICT and biotechnology, the frontier between science and technology is blurring, as fundamental discoveries can lead both to scientific publication and commercial success. Biotechnology companies in particular rely to a very large extent on the science base. A recent analysis of US patent citations found that more than 70% of citations in biotechnology were to papers originating solely at public science institutions (McMillan *et al.*, 2000). A series of studies on the biotechnology industry (Darby *et al.*, 1999) showed that companies' commercial success is closely linked to their connections with the scientific community (*e.g.* the presence of renowned scientists on the board).

The growing role of science in innovation has several causes. First, as noted previously, key technology fields are closely linked to scientific progress. Second, innovation requires more external knowledge and the

Figure 15. **The increasing intensity of science-industry interactions**

University-industry interactions in the United Kingdom (number of papers resulting from collaborative research)

Commercialisation of publicly funded research in the United States (number of publicly funded patents per million dollars of research expenditure)

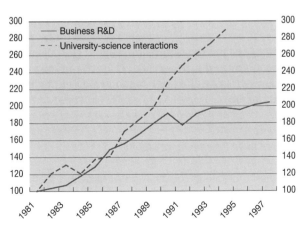
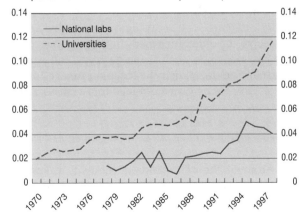

Source: United Kingdom from Katz and Hicks (1998); United States from Jaffe (1999).

decline of corporate laboratories implies that firms need to contract out more research to universities (OECD 1998b).[18] Consequently, business funds an increasing share of university research, including in countries with large R&D spending such as Germany, Japan and the United States. The past decade has seen large increases in Australia, Canada, Finland, Germany, the Netherlands and the United States (OECD, 1999a).

Third, the effect of government policy on the links between science and industry has also been significant. In the United States, the extension of patent protection to publicly funded research has helped to strengthen the role of science in the innovation process (Jaffe, 1999). The science link has also benefited from the introduction of co-operative research and development agreements (CRADAs) between firms and public laboratories. These agreements, which are intended to facilitate technology transfer from the public sector to private industry, have grown rapidly over the 1990s. While the United States was the first to implement such policies, other countries have recently undertaken similar measures (OECD, 2000e). Despite a clear trend towards relaxing regulatory constraints, certain barriers continue to impede the circulation of knowledge between science and industry. One is regulations that affect mobility, *e.g.* non-transferability of pension rights between the public and private sector, as well as employment agreements designed to safeguard trade secrets and proprietary information. Also, evaluation and promotion practices in public research often reduce researchers' incentives to co-operate with the business sector or to engage in academic entrepreneurship.

The importance of the "science link" varies according to countries' industrial specialisation and to the strength of the interaction (including incentives for researchers and enterprises) between the science system and the enterprise sector. In some innovation systems, the link is strong between science and industrial innovation, *e.g.* Canada, Denmark, the United Kingdom and the United States.[19] In others, like Germany, Japan and Korea, but also to a lesser extent in Austria and Italy, innovation has been more geared towards engineering excellence and rapid adoption and adaptation of technological innovation.

Knowledge-intensive business services are of growing importance for innovation

Certain knowledge-intensive business services, such as consultancy, training, R&D and computing services, appear to take a stronger part in innovation, especially in the diffusion process. These services facilitate innovation in other firms, help disseminate innovative concepts and ideas and are an important source of innovation and intangible capital in their own right (Den Hertog and Bilderbeek, 1998). They have highly specialised skills, are important users of IT and are generally regarded as making a significant contribution to diffusion in national innovation systems and thus helping to enhance the economic performance of the system as a whole.[20]

The evidence suggests that these services are gaining in importance and that they are among the economy's most rapidly growing sectors (OECD, 1999e). In the United States, for example, Bureau of Economic Analysis (BEA) data show that the share of business services in the economy doubled from 1980 to 1997, to reach 5.1% of business sector value added. Business services are of increasing value for helping to resolve the difficulties many firms have in incorporating new technologies and adapting to globalisation and new demands, such as the greater complexity of the economy and a growing need for communication (Austrian Federal Ministry of Economic Affairs, 1998). Some growth seems linked to outsourcing, but the bulk seems to reflect growing demand for these services (OECD, 2000b).

Human capital is a key factor in innovation and skilled workers have become more mobile

Although the information economy is accompanied by an increasing codification of knowledge, large amounts of knowledge remain tacit, embodied in people's skills, experience and education. Human capital is therefore crucial to the innovation process, and innovation surveys point to a lack of skilled personnel as one of the greatest barriers to innovation. This is particularly true in the services sector, where innovation is not always related to technology, and where people and the skills they embody help drive innovation

Figure 16. **Researchers per 10 000 in the labour force**
In full-time equivalent

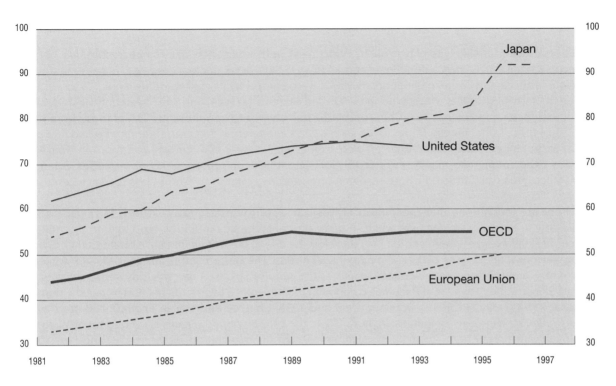

Source: OECD (1999a).

(OECD, 2000b). Certain indicators point to an increasing role for human capital in the economy in general, and in the innovation process in particular (OECD, 1999f):

- The share of researchers and scientists in the labour force continues to increase, particularly outside the United States, as part of a general trend towards upskilling of the labour force (Figure 16).

- Skilled workers and researchers are increasingly mobile across firms and national borders, thereby providing an important contribution to knowledge transfer.

Most of an economy's skill needs are met by the national education system and by business sector training. The OECD Jobs Study stressed the need to improve the effectiveness of the institutions and processes that provide skills and competencies (OECD, 1999g). A properly functioning education and training system helps to equip people with the skills they need to work and participate in society and also helps to match qualifications needed by business and the labour force. Some aspects have become more evident in the 1990s. First, initial levels of education are no longer sufficient in an economy in which demands change continuously; lifelong learning is increasingly important. Second, the skills required by an economy more based on innovation and technological change – creativity, working in teams and cognitive skills – were less needed in the past (Stiglitz, 1999). Third, in some countries, shortages of specific categories of highly skilled personnel, such as ICT workers and scientists and engineers, have emerged in recent years, a potential sign of specific rigidities in these areas. Fourth, owing to the growing importance of personnel mobility for innovation, barriers to mobility and rigidities in education and training systems may inadvertently reduce knowledge flows within an economy.

The domestic market is not always able to meet the demand for skilled workers and engineers. Most OECD economies have therefore, at some point, relied on immigration. Owing to the rapid ageing of the workforce in most OECD countries, some are likely to need to turn again to immigration. While openness to immigration is therefore generally needed, highly skilled personnel, such as good scientists and entrepreneurs, are even more in demand. A country that can attract and retain such people may be at an advantage in an economy where innovation and new firms are necessary to success.

Several factors are likely to play a role in attracting skilled immigrants. Many come as students, but stay to become scientists or start a firm. For example, in 1995, 50% of US doctoral degrees in mathematics and computer science and 58% of engineering degrees were earned by foreign students (NSF, 1998b). In 1995, among the foreign students who stayed in the United States after receiving their degree in 1990-91, about half of the doctoral recipients from China and India had chosen to stay, but only 23% of those from Korea and 28% of those from Chinese Taipei. Of all science and engineering doctoral students who had firm plans to stay in the United States, three-quarters were from Asia, 16% were from Europe and about 6% from North America. Other immigrants may be attracted by job, scientific or entrepreneurial opportunities. Scientists, for instance, are often attracted by the research opportunities offered by world-class research centres.

There are indications that the United States was able to sustain rapid growth in the ICT sector, particularly in the software segment where human capital is the key input, by tapping into international sources of skilled workers. Immigration may therefore be one of the factors that have enabled the US boom to continue, as it filled some of the most urgent skill needs. The United States attracted skilled workers to the country, and US firms went overseas to access the required skills. A recent study shows that nearly a third of Silicon Valley's 1990 workforce was composed of immigrants, two-thirds of them from Asia, primarily China or India (Saxenian, 1999). Between 1995 and 1998, Chinese and Indian engineers started 29% of Silicon Valley's technology companies, up from 13% in the 1980-84 period (Figure 17). A quarter of Microsoft's employees are foreign-born. Australia has also benefited from immigration. Between 1987 and 1999, its net

Figure 17. **Share of Silicon Valley start-ups by ethnic origin (%)**

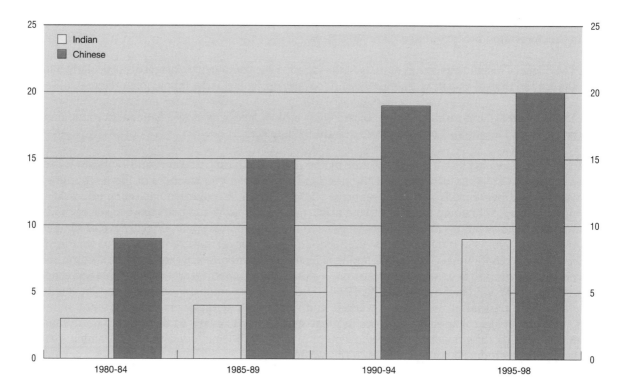

Source: Saxenian (1999).

inflow of scientists and engineers numbered 55 000, of which 27 000 were engineers and 16 000 computer professionals. The net inflow is equivalent to the graduate output of engineers and scientists of five to six Australian universities over the period.

One country's gain often comes at the expense of another's. While systematic international data on the mobility of human resources for science and technology (HRST) do not exist (Carrington and Detragiache, 1998), the largest net loss of scientists and engineers appears to have occurred in non-OECD countries, such as China, India and Russia. India accounts for about 45% of the 115 000 professional work visas granted in the United States each year (Dhume, 2000). Russia has lost 1 000-2 000 employees in the "scientific and science services" sector to emigration during the past years (Gokhberg *et al.*, 2000), the equivalent of 1-2% of total R&D employment. In 1997, 85% of these Russian emigrants went to Germany and Israel. The outflow from these countries may have substantial negative consequences, although in some cases, the "brain drain" becomes a circular flow of human resources with a positive impact, when specialists return with new knowledge, important personal contacts and connections to the global research community. In combination with knowledge of the domestic economy and culture, these can help create new business opportunities.[21]

Shortages of skilled labour in the domestic economy can sometimes also be met by locating facilities abroad, especially for an activity with low fixed costs, such as software. Anecdotal evidence suggests that a number of US firms employed this strategy during the 1990s. Microsoft, Xerox and AT&T all established research centres in the United Kingdom, making software the leader in FDI into the United Kingdom in 1998. In addition, the United States accounts for about half of all software exports from India, much of which is "outsourced" customised work, not finished products. Both India and Israel are home to software development centres for Hewlett-Packard, IBM, Intel, and Microsoft (OECD, 2000c).

The role of ICT in innovation

The above discussion has examined a number of changes that have taken place in the innovation process. In many, ICT plays a major role. First, ICT is the technology area with the highest rate of innovation as measured by patents granted. Among other things, the high rate of patenting in this area points to the many changes in ICT hardware and software that are needed to use ICT effectively. Second, ICT is enabling many of the changes in the economy and the innovation process that help make other economic sectors more innovative. Some aspects of this role, as discussed above, are:

- ICT has helped to break down the natural monopoly character of services such as telecommunication This has enabled regulatory reform, fostered productivity growth and made these services more tradable, so that investment in innovation has increased and they have become more innovative.

- ICT is a key technology for speeding up the innovation process and reducing cycle times, resulting in a closer link between business strategies and performance. For instance, computer simulations of molecular dynamics are proving extremely important in biochemistry and directly affecting drug development. Many prospective drugs can now be identified and if necessary rejected using computer simulations rather than time-consuming testing (OECD, 1998c).

- ICT has fostered greater networking in the economy, as it has facilitated outsourcing and co-operation beyond the firm. It also appears to be a major driver of the globalisation process.

- ICT makes possible faster diffusion of codified knowledge and ideas within and across borders.

- ICT has played an important role in making science more efficient and linking it more closely to business (OECD, 1998c).

The roles of innovation and information technology in recent growth performance are closely related. Some recent changes in the innovation process and related impacts on innovation could not have occurred without ICT. Conversely, some of the impact of information technology might not have been felt in the absence of changes in the innovation system and the economy more broadly. The many and complex links within the economy demonstrate once more that no single factor determines growth. Rather, the economy is a complex and interrelated mechanism, and policies to enhance innovation and growth performance need to address a range of factors. Before discussing some of these policies, the following section examines in greater detail the role of investment in ICT in recent growth performance.

Chapter 3

THE ROLE OF INFORMATION AND COMMUNICATIONS TECHNOLOGY IN GROWTH PERFORMANCE

The impact of investment in information and communications technology on economic growth is commonly regarded as a main driver of the new economy. Over the past 40 years, computer prices have dropped sharply, while their capacity has increased tremendously. Investment has surged, raising the question of how much computers, and more generally, ICT, have contributed to output and labour productivity growth.[22] The United States has been the centre of attention, as the unusual length of its expansion has been associated with strong and sustained rates of investment in ICT (Figure 18). Thus far, its investment in ICT equipment appears to have been more rapid than that of other major OECD regions. In constant (chained 1996) prices, investment in information processing equipment and software as a share of total equipment and software increased from 29% in 1987 to 52% in 1999 (BEA, 2000).

Figure 18. **Private investment in equipment and software in the United States, 1959-99**
Current USD billions

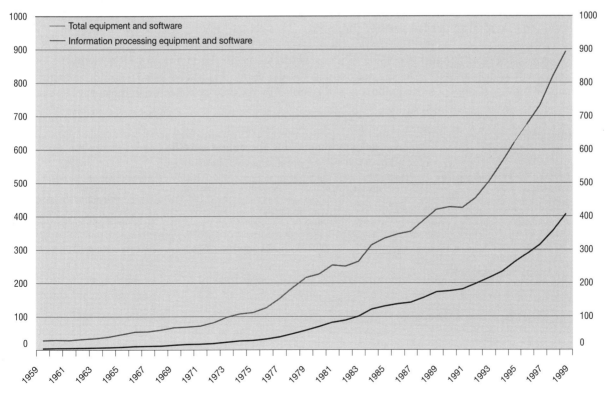

Source: US Bureau of Economic Analysis, March 2000.

In the 1990s, the diffusion of ICT accelerated, especially after 1995. A new wave of ICT, based on applications such as the World Wide Web and the browser, spread rapidly throughout the economy. These Internet-based technologies enable the simultaneous transmission of data, voice, audio and video, thereby vastly increasing the capacity and flexibility of the current communications system, while undercutting the cost and price of traditional modes of transmission. This has contributed to increased demand for ICT equipment and software and transformed small industries into "growth" industries. This new and enhanced infrastructure has also made possible a proliferation of new applications, such as e-mail and electronic commerce, which have fuelled further investment in ICT and supported new business processes, some of which are associated with significant productivity gains.

Evidence on the impact of ICT investment on growth performance emerges from a variety of studies. First, aggregate-level studies provide evidence of the accumulation of ICT capital and of its contribution to output and labour productivity growth. Second, industry and firm-level evidence shows the impact of ICT on business performance in more detail. Third, analysis of the emergence of Internet-based technologies points to new impacts on growth performance. The evidence on the role of Internet on growth performance is limited at this time. The analysis thus relies to a relatively large degree on anecdotal and qualitative information so that, rather than explaining differences in the 1990s, it serves more to indicate potential effects.

The aggregate evidence – significant investment in ICT and a rising contribution to growth

Several studies provide aggregate-level evidence. A recent OECD study, for example, examined the contribution of ICT-producing sectors to output growth across seven OECD countries for the period to 1996 (Schreyer, 2000). It found that technical progress has led to a rapid improvement in the price-performance ratio of ICT capital goods and reduced the user cost of ICT capital goods relative to other types of assets. As a consequence, there has been significant substitution of ICT capital for other types of capital and sustained growth in the volume of investment in ICT, which has outpaced investment in other types of capital goods. Overall, the contribution of ICT capital to output and labour productivity growth has been significant and rising in relative terms. In Canada, the United Kingdom and the United States, ICT equipment contributed about half of fixed capital's contribution to output growth. In France, Germany and Japan, its contribution has been somewhat smaller (Table 3).

However, the study found few signs of an upward change in the trend of MFP growth, the overall efficiency with which combined inputs are used in the economy. An uptake in MFP could be expected if ICT capital provided large positive spillovers and benefits beyond those reflected in the cost of investment

Table 3. **The contribution of ICT to output growth**
Total industries, based on harmonised ICT price index

		Canada	France	Germany	Italy	Japan	United Kingdom	United States
Growth of output:	1980-85	2.8	1.7	1.4	1.4	3.5	2.1	3.4
	1985-90	2.9	3.2	3.6	3.0	4.9	3.9	3.2
	1990-96	1.7	0.9	1.8	1.2	1.8	2.1	3.0
Contributions (percentage points) from:								
ICT equipment	1980-85	0.25	0.17	0.12	0.13	0.11	0.16	0.28
	1985-90	0.31	0.23	0.17	0.18	0.17	0.27	0.34
	1990-96	0.28	0.17	0.19	0.21	0.19	0.29	0.42
Total capital	1980-85	1.3	1.0	1.0	0.9	0.8	0.8	1.1
	1985-90	1.1	1.3	1.2	0.9	1.3	1.1	1.0
	1990-96	0.7	1.0	1.0	0.7	1.0	0.8	0.9

Source: Schreyer (2000).

in ICT. An absence of spillovers implies that returns from the use of ICT have been successfully internalised by ICT producers and users. In addition, firms do not necessarily use ICT to cut costs. If technology allows firms to increase market share at the expense of a competitor, this may simply lead to redistribution rather than to an increase of output at the aggregate level. It may also be that there have been positive effects on MFP which have gone unnoticed because the output has not been measured; the greater convenience of shopping on line, for instance, may not be observed by statistical measures. Finally, spillovers may take some time to materialise.

There are three important limitations to this study. The first is timeliness: the period covered by the analysis ends in 1996, and many new developments in the fast-moving ICT field have taken place since then, notably the spread of the Internet. The second arises from its aggregate perspective: some of the gains in efficiency and productivity from ICT may well be detectable at industry or firm level but cancel out at the level of the entire business sector. For the United States, various approaches have been taken to explore the impact of ICT on productivity performance (Box 3). Third, the analysis was limited to investment in hardware.[23]

Recent data for the United States show an acceleration in MFP growth, with MFP growth rates doubling from about 0.6% over the period 1991-95 to 1.25 % over 1996-99 (Oliner and Sichel, 2000). Jorgenson and Stiroh (2000) confirm these results and argue that technological progress, particularly the rapid advances in semiconductor technology, and capital deepening are the primary factors behind the acceleration in US growth in recent years. It is also increasingly evident in the recent data that the rise in MFP growth is no longer limited to the ICT industry, a possible sign of spillovers from ICT use. While Gordon (1999) still saw a very strong role for the computer industry, recent studies, such as Oliner and Sichel (2000) and the Council of Economic Advisors (2000) find the ICT-producing industry making a much smaller contribution to overall MFP growth (Table 4).[24] Other industries are thus contributing to the increase in MFP, although it is not clear how much is due to the diffusion of ICT to these sectors.

While ICT seems to play a large role in US output and productivity performance, it is unclear to what extent this is the case in other OECD countries. Shinozaki (1999) shows that IT makes a smaller contribution to growth in Japan than in the United States. This appears linked to a slower rate of introduction, with Japanese companies mainly adopting technologies already shown to be effective in the United States, and to a lower volume of investment in ICT. A study for Canada finds that the impact on labour productivity growth of IT investment and of international R&D spillovers linked to import of IT goods is large (Gera *et al.*, 1999). Another study for Canada attributes much of the Canada-US productivity gap in manufacturing to the performance of two sectors, machinery and electronic products, both of which are important producers of IT products (Gu and Ho, 2000).

There appears to be more limited evidence for other OECD countries, partly because the statistical record is less advanced. For Australia, there is evidence that increased productivity has been accompanied

Table 4. **The contribution of the computer industry to US MFP growth**

	Oliner and Sichel (2000)	Council of Economic Advisors (2000)
Period and coverage	Non-farm business sector, 1996-99	Total economy, 1995-99
Annual rate of multi-factor productivity growth	1.25%	1.04%
Annual contribution from the computer industry	0.62% (computer sector plus semiconductor sector)	0.39%
Annual contribution from other industries	0.63%	0.65%

Source: Schreyer (2000).

Box 3. **US productivity performance: the contribution of information and communications technology**

The causes and implications of recent productivity performance in the US economy have been a source of heated debate over the past few years. Official productivity data, from the Bureau of Labor Statistics, indicate that labour productivity growth has been very strong in the past decade and especially in the most recent years. Output per hour in the private non-farm business sector grew at 2% annually over the entire decade and at 2.9% in the 1995-99 period, almost double the average growth rate of the 1973-95 period. The long expansion in the US economy has been accompanied by a surge in investment in ICT assets. There are at least three complementary approaches for assessing the role of ICT in output growth, and different studies of the US economy have covered all three angles:

ICT *industries.* One way to grasp the economic importance of ICT is to look at the importance of ICT production in the economy. Although the share of value added of ICT industries is relatively modest when measured in current prices, the contribution to real output growth can be significant if ICT industries grow faster than other parts of the economy.

ICT *as a capital input.* A second avenue by which ICT can affect output and labour productivity growth is its role as a capital good. ICT investment occurs throughout the economy and thereby provides capital services. These are part of the overall contribution of ICT to output and labour productivity growth. Studies which assess the importance of ICT as a capital input include Jorgenson and Stiroh (2000), Oliner and Sichel (2000), Whelan (2000) and Schreyer (2000). These studies treat ICT capital goods like other types of capital goods; in particular, it is assumed that firms owning ICT assets can reap most or all benefits accruing from using new technologies. Only then is it possible to observe market income accruing to ICT capital and make inferences about its overall contribution to growth. If there are other, unobserved benefits or income, this contribution would be underestimated. This leads to the point about ICT as a special input.

Spillovers from ICT *usage.* A final avenue for tracing effects of ICT involves the claim that ICT produces benefits which go beyond those accruing to investors and owners, for example through network externalities. Where such spillovers exist, they raise overall MFP growth. As such, they are similar to advances in knowledge and new blueprints and formulae or organisational innovations that potentially benefit all market participants. Studies at firm level (for example, Brynjolfsson and Kemerer, 1996; Gandal *et al.*, 1999) do indeed point to spillovers from ICT capital, but it is difficult to transpose these results to the aggregate level.

Notwithstanding such measurement issues, there is growing consensus that ICT has had a strong overall impact on observed output and productivity performance in the United States. While an early study of this issue suggested that much of the rise in overall labour productivity was due to productivity advances in computer-producing industries (Gordon, 1999), this result was not confirmed by later evidence. The latest Economic Report of the President (Council of Economic Advisors, 2000) suggests that only a fraction of the post-1995 acceleration of labour productivity growth is accounted for by the acceleration of MFP in the computer sector. Whelan (2000) and Oliner and Sichel (2000) consider both the direct effect of the productivity boost in the computer-producing industry on aggregate patterns and the indirect impact stemming from the utilisation of computers; they conclude that the overall impact is very strong. More generally, it should also be stressed that the use of different deflators may affect the way in which the overall impact on productivity is split between the ICT-producing industry and the ICT-using industries. For example, the rapid fall in the hedonic ICT deflator in the United States tends to assign a stronger role to the ICT-producing industry.

---

by greater technology use, including ICT (Productivity Commission, 1999). For France, a somewhat different analysis, based on a simulation exercise conducted using the BIPE (*Bureau d'information et de prévision économique*) econometric model, suggests a positive impact of ICT on GDP growth (+2.2% over the next ten years), via increased productivity and supply of new goods and services (SESSI, 1999). In Finland, the electronic equipment industry (which includes the mobile telephone producer, Nokia) contributed three-quarter of a percentage point to annual GDP growth between 1995 and 1999, rising to 1.2 percentage point in 1999 (OECD, 2000f). The Bank of Korea reports that 40% of recent GDP growth in Korea came from the ICT sector, five times its 1999 share in GDP (Yoo, 2000). In the Netherlands, the ICT-producing sector accounted for about 17% of GDP growth over the 1996-98 period, four times its share in GDP (CPB, 2000). For Denmark, Fosgerau and Soresen (1999) find remarkable differences with the United States between sources of growth over the period 1966-98. Productivity growth in Denmark in the recent period is mainly driven by efficiency gains linked to the relocation of factors of production across industries, especially in the agriculture and wholesale and retail sectors. This points to the role played by international trade and specialisation in the growth of a small and open economy such as Denmark, as compared to sustained capital (especially ICT capital) accumulation in the United States. While still sporadic, efforts to measure the contribution of ICT to the economy are improving and suggest that the phenomenon is not limited to the United States.

Evidence at industry and firm level

The industry level: ICT increases productivity in using industries

The previous section showed that, at least in the United States, some ICT-using sectors are now observing a pick-up in MFP growth, a possible sign of spillover effects from ICT use. Although computers may appear to be everywhere, the use of ICT is actually highly concentrated in the services sector and in a few manufacturing sectors (Figure 19) (McGuckin and Stiroh, 1998). ICT is particularly important for certain services sectors, because many services are concerned with the processing and diffusion of information.[25] This is particularly true for sectors such as financial services, communication and public administration. Advances in ICT, which allow more information to be codified and increasingly move towards knowledge technologies, such as expert systems, have expanded the scope for ICT use in many services. In sectors dealing with more physical services, such as transport and distribution, ICT is often integrated in

Figure 19. **Relative IT intensity index by industry[1] in the United States, 1997**

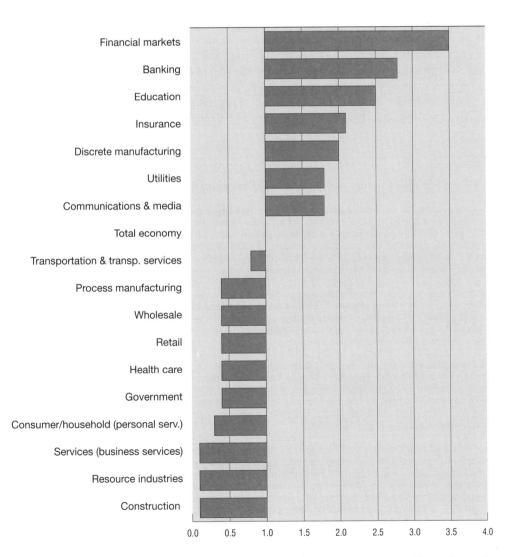

1. The relative IT intensity index represents an industry's percentage share of information technology expenditures relative to its share of GDP. An index of 1 reflects no over- or under-spending in IT relative to the size of the industry.
Source: OECD (2000c), based on data from the US Bureau of Economic Analysis and IDC.

technologies that improve logistics and automate complex processes such as systems integration, which is a key cost element in industries such as aircraft and motor vehicles. In human and social services, such as medical and health services, ICT is also increasingly used. Some of the evidence on services sector R&D also show its importance (OECD, 1997b). About a third of R&D carried out in the services sector is IT-related and concerns software development or computer services. Innovation surveys, such as the recent German survey, suggest that personal computers, office software, communication networks, data banks and specialised software are the key technologies for many service firms (Mannheim Innovation Panel, 1999).

Services sectors have made significant contributions to productivity growth in certain OECD Member countries. For example, productivity gains in the distribution sector have been relatively rapid over the past decade (OECD, 2000b). A key factor in these gains has been the greater use of advanced technologies, particularly ICT (Reardon *et al.*, 1996; Broersma and McGuckin, 1999). These include scanning and inventory management systems, greater use of self-service systems, increases in scale and closer integration of manufacturers and retailers. Since the mid-1980s, ICT has led to considerable shifts in retail practices in the United States, where lean retailing resulted in the integration of enterprises at all stages of the distribution and production chain (Abernathy *et al.*, 1999).

Nevertheless, the overall contribution of market services to labour productivity growth remains quite limited in many countries. However, slow productivity growth in services masks a wide variety of experience and is affected by measurement problems (Box 4). In some services, such as trucking, health services, financial services and business services, technological change has strongly affected the production process and the organisation of production and has contributed to significant improvements in productivity, but these may not always be easy to measure. For example, trucking firms are using advances in telecommunication technologies to make real-time operations information available to a dispersed transportation network. Increasingly, communication in support of trade between firms uses some means of electronic data

---

Box 4. Problems for measuring output and productivity

Capturing price declines in information and communication technology goods. Whenever products experience rapid quality changes, statistical agencies face the problem of accurately appreciating price changes in goods. Computers are a good example: their quality, in terms of computing power, speed, etc., evolves rapidly, with new models replacing old ones on the market. Price statistics are based on a comparison of the same good between two points in time, and, with rapid turnover, like is no longer compared with like. Practices vary in dealing with this situation, and different methods can lead to a widely different appreciation of the evolution of computer prices (OECD, 1996).

A related problem arises when there is a lag between the appearance of a new product and its inclusion in the basket of goods underlying a price index. Price declines that occur during this period are not captured and may lead to overestimation. Hausman (1997) looks at cellular phones and shows how the delayed inclusion of this new consumer good potentially affects price indices and thus the measurement of the economy's real output. When inclusion lags differ among countries, they may hinder international comparison.

Measuring output in services. Achieving a suitable measure of services output over time is complicated by two factors: i) market prices may not be observable for publicly provided services; and ii) it may be difficult to identify the service activity precisely and to account correctly for quality changes. It is necessary to identify whether the output consists of the transaction or the outcome from the service. For example, should teaching output be measured by numbers of teaching hours or by results achieved by students? In the first case, productivity growth is zero by definition. In the second, productivity rises when students improve their marks.

If the change in quality of a good or service is ignored in measuring quantity, all price changes (including those due to quality changes) will be registered as inflationary moves, and what is being compared over time will not be truly comparable. As a consequence, real output will be undervalued. Differences in quality of services are often difficult to observe. For example, measuring the hours spent by a lawyer with clients is straightforward, but it is very difficult to measure the quality of the advice given. Yet its quality is a determinant of the price of the service, and a price rise due to greater probability of winning a case cannot be distinguished from price rises for other reasons. Current statistical practices are ill-equipped to deal with this issue and tend to vary among countries. Another difficulty is to identify the individual elements that usually compose a service. The banking sector, for example, offers a whole series of services such as safekeeping, accounting or facilitating payment of bills. These functions are difficult to seize in statistical practice, and proxies, such as number of transactions, accounts or outstanding credits, have to be used.

interchange (EDI). The Internet is now combined with EDI to offer innovative improvements in service. This reduces costs and delays and increases the reliability of information exchange. It also leads to greater customer satisfaction, creation of new markets and changes in business models and processes. The biggest process innovation made by trucking firms was to absorb the logistics function into their value chain. In the United States, this has contributed to the rapid development of the logistics business (Nagarajan *et al.*, 1999).

Efforts to improve measurement of the output of various services on a sector-by-sector basis typically result in upward revisions of these sectors' productivity. For example, Fixler and Zieschang (1999) introduce quality adjustments to capture the effects of improved service characteristics, such as easier and more convenient transactions and intermediation, made possible by new technology in the US financial services industry. These improvements caused output to grow by over 7% a year between 1977 and 1994, well above the traditionally computed measure which only rose by 1.3% over the same period.[26] Other studies show similar results for the health care and trucking industries when price measures are developed to capture some of this sector's quality changes (for an example applied to the treatment of depression, see Frank *et al.*, 1998; for transport, see Chakraborty and Kazarosian, 1999).

*The firm level: **ICT** improves productivity by enabl,ing organisational innovation*

The greatest benefits from ICT appear to be realised when ICT investment is combined with other organisational assets, such as new strategies, new business processes, new organisational structures and better worker skills. Unlike some other "general purpose technologies", the successful integration of ICT requires significant structural adjustment, as the experience of the past decades demonstrates. ICT facilitates sharing and co-ordination of information among different parties, thus reducing the need for middle-level managers while fostering an organisational structure of semi-independent groups linked laterally rather than vertically (Lipsey, 1999). This reduces the need for these units to be a formal part of the firm and allows firms to outsource activities and concentrate on their core competence. In the extreme, this leads to a form of firm organisation in which constellations of various firms combine to work on a particular project and then disband (Malone and Laubacher, 1998).

While this organisational form may not become prevalent, it is clear that a significant amount of experimentation is under way, much of it driven by firms responding to the technological opportunities offered by ICT. In a recent US survey, a quarter of all firms reported that they have made organisational changes to respond to the changes wrought by the Internet (NABE, 2000). At firm level, many studies have found that ICT has a positive impact on firm performance when its introduction is associated with complementary organisational change (Table 5). Because organisational change tends to be firm-specific, it is not surprising that these studies show on average a positive return to ICT investment, but with a huge variation across organisations (Brynjolfsson and Hitt, 1997).

The studies mentioned in Table 5 primarily look at the role of ICT in individual firm performance. However, the emergence of networks, such as the Internet, increasingly underscores the need to broaden the focus to a product's entire value chain, particularly a firm's interaction with suppliers and customers. Supply chain management is the optimisation of goods and service supply within the value chain by making sales and production information available to all enterprises in that chain. While the concept has existed for some time, the information infrastructure that makes it possible to integrate management across the value chain has not (ECOM, 1999).

The widespread use of enterprise resource planning (ERP) software in recent years has allowed real-time production and procurement planning, while the use of EDI makes possible the integration of receipt and placement of orders between customer and supplier. These technologies have helped to reduce inventories and the costs of procurement, storage and transport.[27] The new AutoXchange, developed by the "Big 3" US auto makers but open to manufacturers in other sectors and countries, is projected to connect at least 30 000 suppliers, with cost savings of about 20%.[28] On an aggregate basis, US durable goods manufacturers reduced inventories as a share of sales by more than a quarter between 1989 and 1999. This

Table 5. **Selected firm-level studies on ICT, productivity and organisational change**

Study	Sample	Issue addressed	Main findings
Lichtenberg (1995)	US firms, 1988-91	Output contribution of capital and labour deployed in information systems	One information systems employee can be substituted for six non-information systems employees without affecting output
Hitt and Brynjolfsson (1997); Brynjolfsson and Hitt (1997)	More than 600 large US firms, 1987-94	The impact of the adoption of IT and organisational decentralisation on productivity	Firms that both adopt IT and organisational decentralisation are on average 5% more productive than those that adopt only one of these
Black and Lynch (1997 and 2000)	US firms, 1987-93, and 1993 and 1996	The impact of workplace practices, IT and human capital on productivity	The adoption of certain newer work practices, higher educational levels, and the use of computers by production workers have a positive impact on plant productivity
Brynjolfsson and Yang (1998)	Fortune 1000 US firms, 1987-94	The impact of IT and intangible assets on firm performance	The market value of USD 1 of IT capital is the same as that of USD 10 of capital stock. This may reflect the value of intangible investment associated with ICT
Brynjolfsson, Hitt and Yang (1998)		The impact of the adoption of IT and organisational decentralisation on productivity	The market value of USD 1 of IT capital is higher by USD 2-5 in decentralised firms
Bresnahan, Brynjolfsson and Hitt (1999)	400 large firms, 1987-96	Complementarity between IT investment, human capital and decentralised organisational structure	IT combined with work practices such as higher skills, greater educational attainment, greater use of delegated decision making lead to a higher value of IT investment.

Source: OECD summary.

does not take into account savings associated with not having to finance those inventories, warehouse them and discount them to accommodate shifts in demand (US Department of Commerce, forthcoming).

The second area of possible benefits concerns customer relationships. Integrated customer management makes possible greater efficiency in the supplier-customer relationship, reducing costs, increasing convenience and broadening the customer base. For example, the cost of customer service telephone reception can drop from 7% to 1% of the cost of a bank's office management, if a voice response unit can be used. Also, products can be better handled, services can be expanded, consumer purchasing behaviour can be analysed to increase efficiencies in the marketing processes. In addition, the entire demand flow can be automated and reduce personnel costs (ECOM, 1999).

A new role for ICT in the 1990s?

Firm-level evidence confirms that ICT can have a strong impact on labour productivity. However, some macroeconomic and microeconomic evidence for the United States suggests that, particularly in the latter half of the 1990s, the role of ICT may have evolved and affect multi-factor productivity as well, for three main reasons. First, the 1990s saw various regulatory reforms which led to further liberalisation of the telecommunication sector; this has helped to increase competition, reduce costs and enhance innovation. Second, technological innovations of the 1990s, *e.g.* fibre optics, high capacity and high speed hard disk drives, digital subscriber line (DSL) technologies and satellite technologies, greatly increased the volume and capacity of communications. Third, and probably most important, convergence of the telecommunication and information technology sectors accelerated in 1994-95 with the emergence of the Internet's key infrastructure applications, the World Wide Web and the browser (Figure 20), which greatly expanded the potential of ICT. At relatively low cost, these technologies linked the existing capital stock of computers and communications systems in an open network that significantly increased their utility.

It is probably too early to observe clearly the impact of these more recent technological and regulatory changes on aggregate productivity data, although the most recent US data may already point to the impact of ICT on MFP. However, anecdotal and qualitative information strongly suggests that the nature and speed of diffusion of ICT are changing, with profound impacts on all sectors of the economy and all actors in society. These factors differentiate newer information and communications technologies (*i.e.* the Internet) from previous ones:

- The Internet is more pervasive and is diffusing faster. This is partly due to rapidly decreasing ICT prices which have fallen more rapidly in the 1990s. The US quality-adjusted index for computers shows a drop of almost 90% in producer prices of personal computers (PCs), workstations and laptops over a six-year period, compared to a decline of 40% for large-scale computers. More recent data on US consumer prices for various ICT goods and services confirm the sharp decline in the cost of both PCs and information processing services, which dropped by 43% and 32%, respectively, over the past two years (Figure 21).

- The Internet's most profound economic impact is not necessarily associated with the new "dot.com" start-ups but rather with the effect it is having on existing industries that are adopting ICT and restructuring to exploit the new technology. In agriculture, it is providing better information about market prices and has fostered the emergence of new online commodity markets. In construction, the Internet reduces the need for blueprints and allows seamless communication among subcontractors. In

Figure 20. **Growth in Internet host computers and major e-commerce developments**

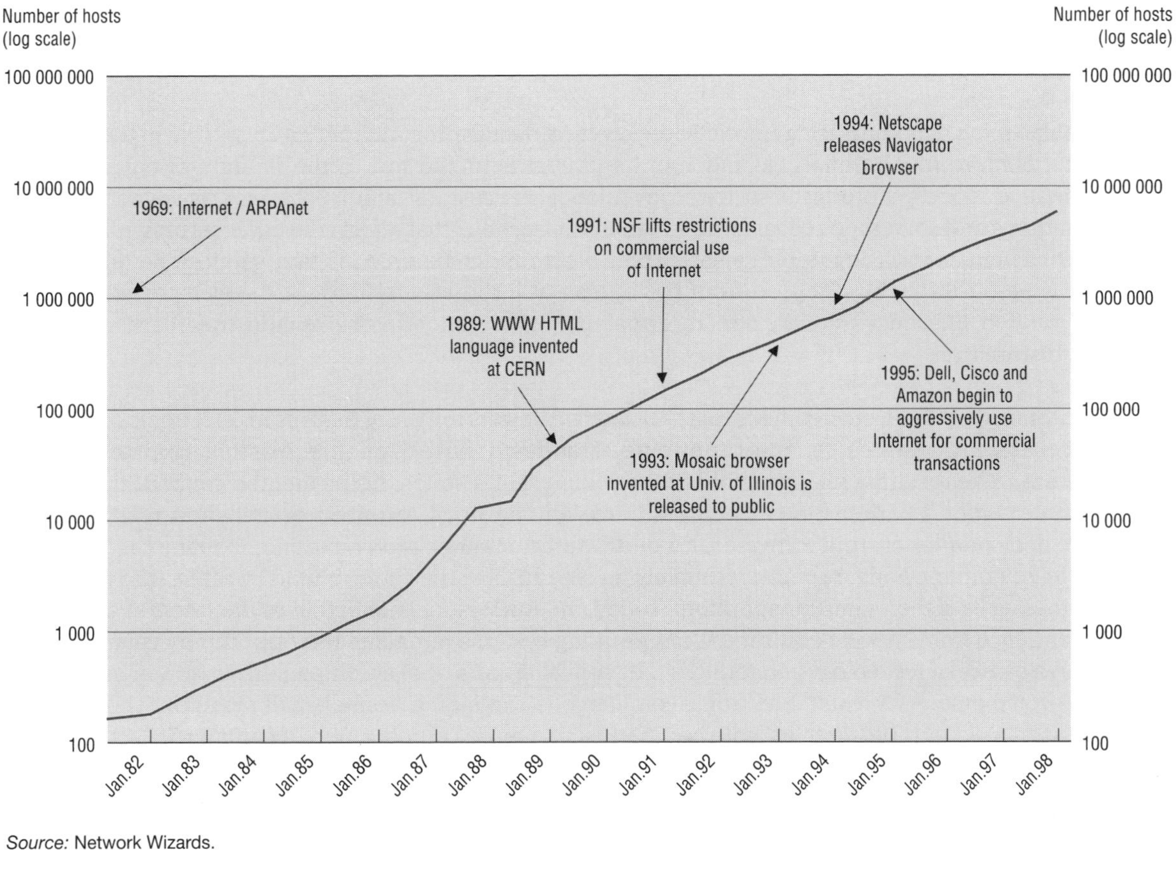

Source: Network Wizards.

Figure 21. **US consumer price index for selected ICT equipment and services[1]**
December 1997 = 100 (not seasonally adjusted)

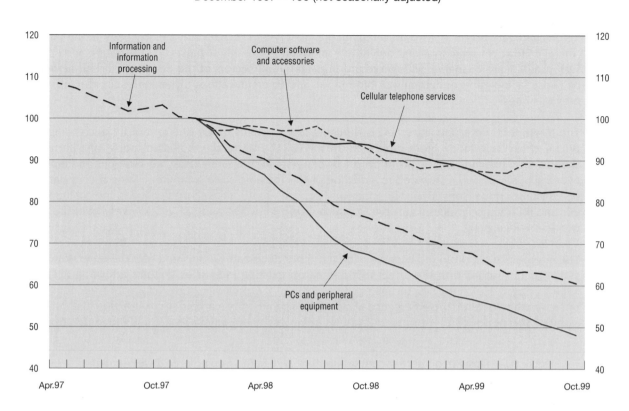

1. Information and information processing, excluding telephone services.
Source: US Bureau of Labor Statistics (BLS), November 1999.

manufacturing, it is generating new efficiencies by reducing procurement costs. Its role in the services sector is more revolutionary, as much of its impact is linked not to the volume of output but to qualitative aspects of products, such as convenience and customisation. Such aspects are not captured in statistics and sometimes occur as non-market transactions that affect consumer surplus, *e.g.* Internet banking from home. The Internet also enables electronic commerce in many services, so that sectors that were traditionally shielded from the effects of international trade are now more exposed to competition. Efficiency gains are already apparent in information-intensive industries, such as banking and distribution.

The Internet creates an environment that substantially lowers the entry barriers for electronic commerce, in part because it adheres to non-proprietary standards based on the existing communications infrastructure.[29] The resulting low threshold for both buyers and sellers helps fuel the continued growth of the Internet market.[30] Earlier forms of e-commerce among firms required established relationships, expensive and complex custom software, and dedicated communication links and, in many cases, strictly compatible equipment. Early e-commerce mainly involved EDI and electronic fund transfers (EFT) between large businesses and their first-tier suppliers. Today, the low cost of connecting to the Internet along with its independence from specific equipment or operating systems mitigates the opportunity costs of being locked into a particular technology and reduces the "switching costs" that accompanied the adoption of earlier forms of e-commerce. As a result, electronic commerce is expanding from a small range of EDI business-to-business transactions between established parties to a more complex web of commercial activity.

While electronic commerce is still in an embryonic state, where its impact on aggregate activity may be hard to detect, its use is already widespread and diffusing rapidly. For large firms, Internet access is

Figure 22. **Internet penetration rate in the business sector in selected OECD countries**
Most recent year

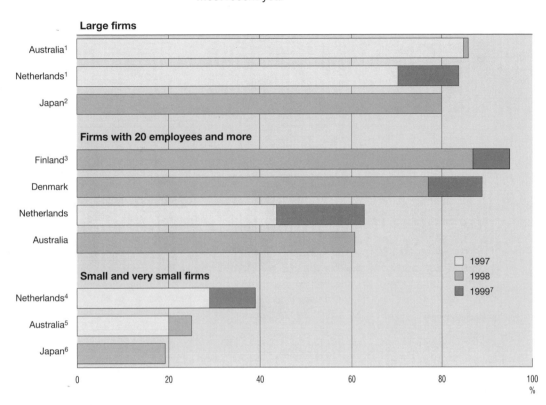

1. Firms with 200 employees and more.
2. Firms with 300 employees and more.
3. Among firms already using information technologies
4. Firms with less than 10 employees.
5. Firms with less than 5 employees.
6. Firms with less than 6 employees.
7. 1999 are forecasts.
Source: National statistical sources: ABS (Australia), Statistics Denmark (Denmark), MPT (Japan), Statistics Netherlands (Netherlands) and Statistics Finland (Finland).

becoming nearly universal and even for small firms the penetration is relatively high and rapidly increasing (Figure 22). In countries like Denmark and Finland that have attempted to measure e-commerce through the Internet systematically, over half of the enterprises with more than 20 employees started to make orders using the Internet in 1999, up from about 15% in 1997. And about 40% of firms received orders in 1999, up from just 7% in 1997 (Statistics Denmark and Statistics Finland, 2000).

Electronic commerce technologies provide a faster, more reliable and potentially more cost-effective way to connect firms, making existing business processes between firms more efficient. These technologies, especially when applied to business-to-business relations, may lead to significant productivity gains for two reasons. First, e-commerce technologies are relatively cheap and make possible the automation of relatively simple, but ubiquitous processes such as distribution, sales, after-sales service and inventory management. Internet solutions have been primarily developed for distribution channel management, while supply chain management is typically carried out through EDI applications. However, as its costs decline, the Internet is likely to be increasingly used for supply management processes by new entrants and small companies that cannot afford EDI (Figure 23). Second, to be effective, e-commerce technologies need to be applied all along the business value chain in an integrated fashion. This significantly broadens the uses of the Internet throughout the economy.

Figure 23. **The diffusion of Internet-based applications**
Percentage of new low-end Internet business-to-business projects, by business process
Worldwide, 1997-2003

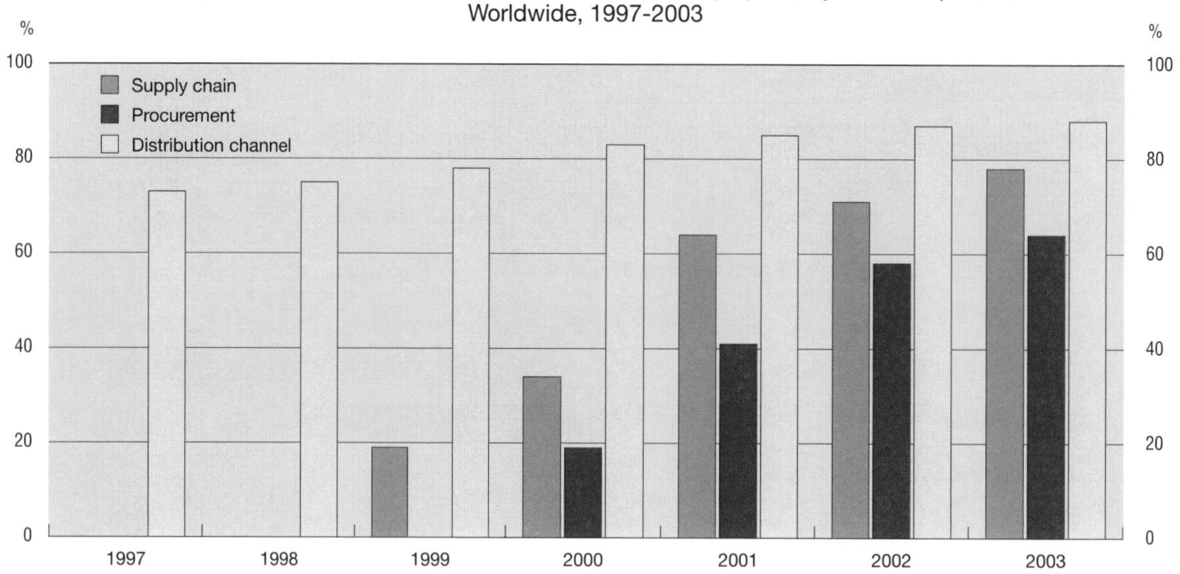

Source: Datamonitor (1999).

General purpose Internet-based applications can thus be used across a vast range of sectors. In the United States, the impact of the Internet can already be observed among early adopters of e-commerce technologies. There is evidence of improved collaboration in the design of products (shorter design processes, increased product customisation, greater standardisation of parts) and in production and logistics (lower inventory costs, faster production, lower supply costs) (Box 5).

Business-to-business applications offer potential cost savings on both the supply and the demand side. The impact on costs depends on the cost structure of individual firms and is thus to some extent industry-specific. Firm-level case studies, mainly for the United States, provide some evidence on average cost reductions across industries. However, cost reductions are not limited to typical e-commerce firms, such as Cisco, Dell, E*Trade and Charles Schwab. Evidence of more widespread cost reductions is emerging, as business-to-business trade over the Internet spreads throughout the US economy.

Estimates of potential cost reductions from electronic commerce are not yet universally available, owing to the relative maturity of the e-commerce market in different countries. In the United States, where electronic commerce is already well developed, firm-level evidence points to considerable reductions in

Table 6. **Potential cost savings from business-to-business e-commerce in the United States**

Industry	Potential cost savings	Industry	Potential cost savings
Electronic components	29-39%	Chemicals	10%
Machinings (metals)	22%	MRO	10%
Forest products	15-25%	Communications/bandwidth	5-15%
Freight transport	15-20%	Oil and gas	5-15%
Life science	12-19%	Paper	10%
Computing	11-20%	Health care	5%
Media and advertising	10-15%	Food ingredients	3-5%
Aerospace machinings	11%	Coal	2%
Steel	11%		

Source: Goldman Sachs (1999).

product and process costs across sectors (Table 6). Although they vary across industries, product costs are estimated to represent, on average, 50-70% of the total cost of intermediate goods, with process costs making up the rest. Business-to-business solutions are estimated to reduce process costs by 10-25% and product costs by more than 20%. Depending on the cost structure, this translates into an overall cost reduction of 13-22%. Recent estimates by Goldman Sachs suggest that this would means an overall increase of 5% in GDP. A recent report on Australia estimates that GDP may be 2.7% higher in 2007 if e-commerce practices are widely adopted (NOIE, 2000). A study for Japan found that the greatest returns from investing

---

Box 5. Main efficiency gains from e-commerce applications

The cost of executing a sale. The electronic interface allows e-commerce traders to verify the internal consistency of an order and to match order, receipt and invoice. This process may seem trivial, but both General Electric (GE) and Cisco report that one-quarter of their orders previously had to be reworked because of errors. At Cisco, the use of electronic commerce for ordering – instead of phone, fax or e-mail – has automated the verification procedure and reduced the error rate to 2%. To address the problem, GE has developed a Trading Post Network (TPN). It allows requisitions to be posted electronically for outside bids by any supplier and has significantly reduced the error rate in orders. It has also generated other benefits, such as a 5-20% drop in materials costs due to increased supplier competition and a 50% reduction in the procurement cycle (Margherio *et al.*, 1998).

Customer support and after-sales services. In economies characterised by sophisticated products, customer service and after-sales service are a major cost for many firms, often accounting for more than 10% of operating costs. Electronic commerce allows firms to move much of this support on line. Customers can access databases or "smart" manuals directly; this significantly cuts costs while often improving the quality of service. Cisco, the largest supplier of routers for Internet traffic, had moved 70% of its customer support on line by 1997, including manuals, software and employee recruitment procedures (Meeker, 1997). This aggressive use of electronic commerce eliminated an estimated quarter million phone calls a month and saved over USD 500 million, which represented about 9% of total revenue or 17% of total operating costs (Margherio *et al.*, 1998).

Purchase orders and procurement. Even when the actual transaction takes place outside the firm, there are significant internal costs associated with procurement. The purchase order of a low-value requisition for office supplies or travel may take between USD 80 and USD 125 to process, often exceeding the value of the material (Margherio *et al.*, 1998). The high cost of procurement is linked to the error-prone and time-consuming process that is often required to control purchasing costs, including its route through several departments. Internet-based e-commerce enables the application of EDI-type systems to relatively small purchases, reduces the error rate, can ensure compliance with organisational norms and speeds up the process. Estimates of the savings generated range from 10% to 50%, although the largest savings are often not monetary (Girishankar, 1997). For instance, MCI reports that the use of e-commerce to buy PCs reduced its computer purchase cycle from 4-6 weeks to 24 hours (Margherio *et al.*, 1998). Bell South cut the approval time for expense reports from three weeks to two days (Davis, 1998), and the US General Services Administration (GSA) more than halved the time needed to complete a purchase, by replacing its EDI system with an Internet-based system (Girishankar, 1997).

Inventories. Directly linked to time savings associated with procurement are savings in inventory costs: the faster an input can be ordered and delivered, the less need for a large inventory. In the United States, the average value of non-farm inventories represents some 2.3% of annual final sales and 4.2% of sales of final goods. Approximately 37% of all inventories are "carried" by manufacturers, while 25% and 27% of total non-farm inventories are held by wholesale and retail trade, respectively. Each stage of the value-added chain therefore holds considerable inventories. For retailers, the cost of carrying an inventory for a year is estimated to be equivalent to at least 25% of what they receive in payment for the product (Taylor, 1997). A two-week reduction in inventory thus represents a cost saving of 1% of sales. As most retailers operate on margins of 3 to 4%, this is quite significant.

Forecasting consumer demand. A key factor in reducing inventory costs is greater ability to forecast demand. E-commerce firms that allow consumers to customise their order or select from a wide variety of choices obtain valuable information on consumer preferences. This improves their ability to forecast demand. In a traditional store, a consumer might buy a computer with unwanted features or lacking certain features because the desired model was not available. In this situation, the merchant is ignorant of the consumer's true preferences. An e-commerce trader that offers a "build-to-order" computer, instead, knows exactly what consumers prefer and can adjust the product line accordingly. In addition, the links that electronic commerce provides along the supply chain make it possible to pass this information on to partners, thereby lowering their costs and probably overall costs. This practice, known as collaborative planning forecasting replenishment (CPFR), has been estimated to lead to a reduction in overall inventories of USD 250-350 billion, or about 20-25% of current US inventory levels (Ernst & Young, cited in Margherio *et al.*, 1998). While this estimate seems optimistic, pilot studies in the US auto market obtained 20% savings. Even a 5% reduction would have significant economic impact. Gains can also be achieved by having stock that matches customers' needs more closely. Japanese supermarkets like Sotetsu Rosen have used this technique, eliminating out-of-stock items (Ministry of Trade and Industry, 1998).

Source: OECD (1999h).

---

in technologies supporting electronic commerce can be realised in supply chain management and customer management. The estimated rates of return for these two types of investment ranged between 200% and 400% in the medium term (three to five years), and 600% and 800% in the longer term (five to ten years). Cost effectiveness appears particularly high in process manufacturing (foods and processed goods, publishing and printing) and services where e-commerce can facilitate operations (*e.g.* financial services, wholesale and retail distribution) (ECOM, 1999).

Reaping the benefits from new ICT: are OECD economies on divergent paths?

The diffusion and impact of ICT are, to a certain extent, firm-, sector- and country-specific. Even if countries had similar rates of ICT investment or diffusion, this would not necessarily mean that ICT had a comparable effect on performance. For instance, the average ICT intensity of fast-growing and slow-growing countries does not seem to be significantly different (OECD, 1999a). This partly hides differences in the implementation of ICT. At the firm level, it is not only the size of the investment that matters, but also the way in which ICT investment is complemented by organisational change and investment in human capital. At the aggregate level, countries' ability to respond to rapid technological change greatly depends on the availability of key factors, such as the right set of skills and well-functioning product and capital markets – elements discussed earlier in this report. Collectively, these factors create an environment that is conducive to innovation and receptive to new technologies such as ICT. The most recent evidence on the US economy points to the strong positive impact of ICT on economic growth and performance, probably enabled by the "right" environment. The previous section identified some of the channels through which the new technological "wave" could have a greater impact on economic and productivity growth, *e.g.* use of the Internet and applications like e-commerce. This section looks at differences in the level and rate of adopting Internet-based technologies across OECD countries, so as to provide an indication of the technological lags that may exist between countries. Even if these lags are eliminated, however, the nature of the impact of ICT on productivity will depend on broader framework conditions.

The Internet is not any one system or device but is rather a "network of networks". It uses software, communication protocols and routing and switching devices to link together a number of different terminal devices (PCs, phones, TVs) to a variety of communication channels, including broadcasting, various cable systems, telephone networks, value-added networks and local or wide area networks. Thus, comparing the state of its development across countries requires examination of all these elements.

The first of these is the telecommunications infrastructure. Investment in telecommunication networks in OECD countries reached a record USD 151 billion in 1997, with mobile investment accounting for 26% of the total (Figure 24). The largest single increase was in the United States (OECD, 1999i). New investments in the communications infrastructure are being made to increase the capacity of the communications network (high-capacity bandwidth), by adding fibre optic cables, second phone lines and high-speed access services (*e.g.* ISDN, DSL). These investments respond to growing demand for Internet access, which in turn generates new demand for longer calls, second residential lines, higher-speed, high-quality services (*e.g.* ISDN) and leased lines. For example, US inter-exchange carriers increased the amount of fibre optic cable, as measured by fibre miles, by 21% in 1998. The opening of local access markets to competition has also driven large investment increases in countries such as Australia and the United Kingdom (OECD, 1999i). New markets are also appearing for faster and wider Internet access, for improved Web content hosting (the maintenance and development of content over the World Wide Web), for expanded private intranets and extranets and for a global infrastructure for electronic commerce (including electronic payment, authentication, etc.) (OECD, 2000c).

In addition to the communications infrastructure, critical elements of the Internet include software that links the various components and ICT services, such as systems integrators. These are currently the most dynamic components of the ICT infrastructure. While their development depends partly on country-specific factors, standards and network externalities play a key role. The most obvious explanation for the leading position of the US software industry is that it has enjoyed a first-mover advantage in all market segments

Figure 24. **Telecommunications investment by region, 1985-97**

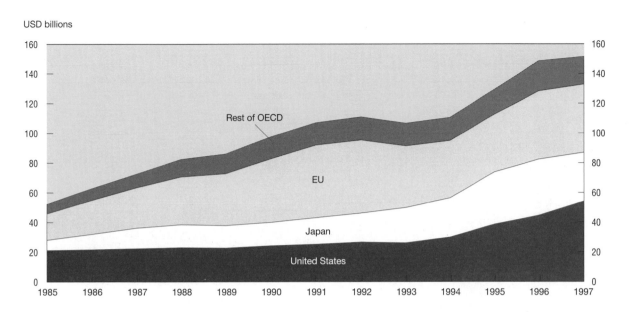

Source: OCDE (1999i).

of the software industry (Figure 25). Computer production and rates of use in Europe and Japan have lagged behind, leaving domestic software producers with smaller markets and limited economies of scale.

First-mover advantages also reflect US government R&D support and procurement for defence purposes, the early development of computer science education in US universities, antitrust decisions that unbundled software from hardware, favourable patent policy and the existence of a vibrant venture capital market (Mowery, 1996; Anchordoguy, 2000). The success of the United States in these areas may also be linked to the close proximity of producers and demanding users in a large domestic market (Mowery, 1999).

Comparable statistics on the terminal devices uses to access the Internet remain somewhat limited, but the use of PCs is one important indicator as is mobile phone use since new standards will allow access to the Web. Figure 26 shows the average PC installed base which differs considerably across the OECD area, with the United States showing a large and increasing lead *vis-à-vis* the seven largest OECD countries, followed by some smaller ones. As Figure 27 indicates, the use of mobile phones is more prevalent in many European and Asian countries than in the United States. This may provide an opportunity to spread Internet access to a large portion of the population, and could help to close the gap in access that exists across countries.

The leading position of the United States in many of these areas has meant that it enjoys a leading position *vis-à-vis* other OECD countries in terms of computers ("hosts") linked to the Internet. In September 1999, the host penetration rate for the United States was three times the average for the OECD area, seven times that of the European Union and just over eight times that of Japan. Between 1999 and March 2000, the United States added an additional 25.1 Internet hosts per 1 000 inhabitants, compared to an additional 5.5 Internet hosts for the United Kingdom, 4.1 for Japan, 3.0 for Germany and 2.7 for France (OECD, 2000g). In short, instead of other countries catching up to the United States, the gap appears to be widening.

This combination of factors – modern communications infrastructure, strong software and computer services industries and a large user base – provide a supportive environment for Internet applications like

Figure 25.   **Packaged software markets, 1990-97**
Value in USD billions and growth in percentage

G7 countries

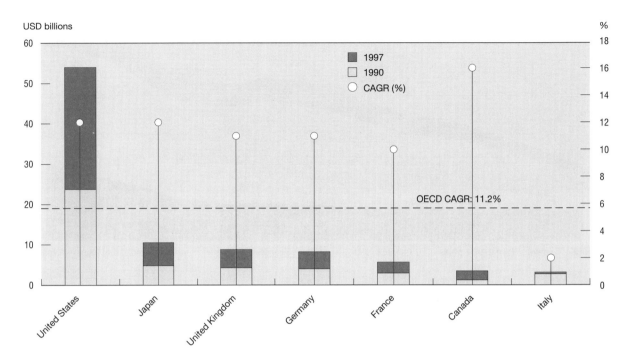

Other OECD

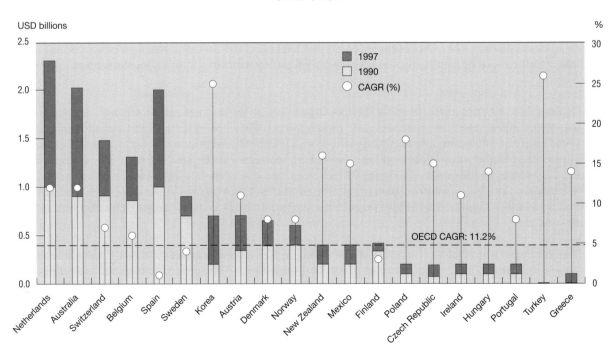

Source: OECD, Information Technology Outlook 2000.

OECD 2000

Figure 26. **Average PC installed base in the OECD area, 1992[1] and 1997**

G7 countries

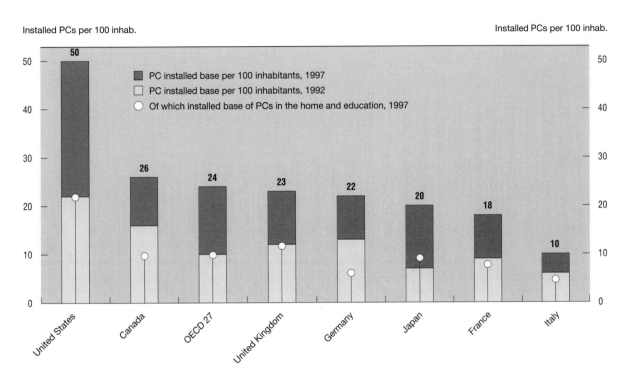

Other OECD

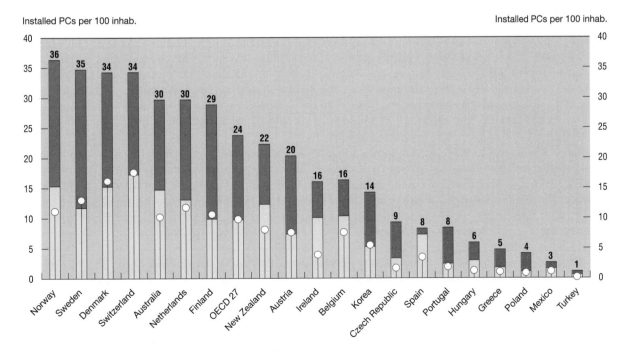

1. Total PC installed base divided by total population. For some countries, 1994 instead of 1992.
Source: OECD, *Information Technology Outlook 2000.*

Figure 27. **Cellular mobile subscribers per 100 inhabitants, June 1999**

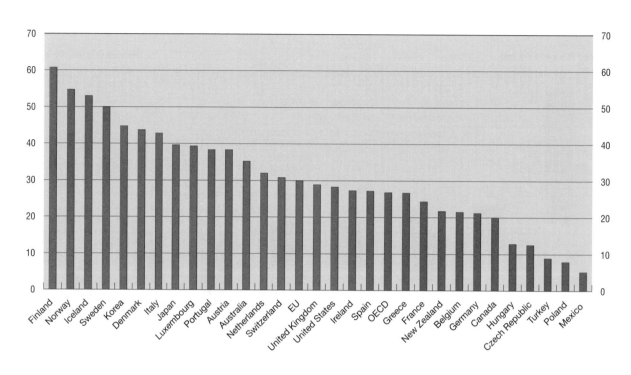

Source: OECD (2000h).

electronic commerce. One measure of this is the diffusion of Web servers that have been configured to handle "secure" activity such as transactions involving payment by credit card. As of March 2000, the United States had six times as many secure servers per capita as the European Union, nine times more than France, eleven times more than Japan and sixteen times more than Italy. Even the Nordic countries, traditionally leaders in communication infrastructure, are currently lagging behind the OECD average (OECD, 2000g). The most recent data show that, over the past years, the United States has been expanding its lead. It seems to be currently enjoying a virtuous circle, linked to network effects, in which demand for and supply of Internet-based services and electronic commerce are mutually reinforcing (Figure 28).

Part of this growth in secure servers comes from abroad. Because it enjoys a competitive position in terms of as provider of Internet access, software and services, the United States has also become a hub for online content. For example, four of the top ten most accessed Web sites under the top level domain name **.fr** are physically located in Sweden, Germany and the United States. These same countries also host five of the top ten Web sites under **.uk**. The location of Web sites in the United States and some other OECD countries is due to large cost differences (OECD, 2000g).

What these trends point to is the increasing role played by demand-side economies of scale. While earlier ICT applications required established relationships, expensive and complex custom software, and dedicated communication links, the Internet network is independent of any one platform and its economic value is closely linked to the number of firms and households connected to it. Consequently, the first player to enter benefits from positive network externalities on a global scale and can acquire an advantage in terms not only of branding and reputation but also of economies of scale.

One prospect for capturing the beneficial properties of network externalities is to exploit the use of wireless devices to close the gap with the United States. To do so, however, a number of challenges will

Figure 28. **Growth of secure servers**
Secure servers per million inhabitants

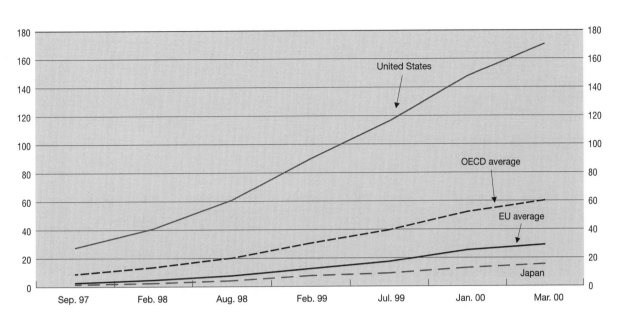

Note: The population data used for February 1999 to March 2000 refer to 1999.
Source: OECD (www.oecd.org/dsti/sti/it/cm) based on Netcraft (www.netcraft.com).

have to be addressed. One is the limited amount of spectrum currently allocated to wireless transmissions and the challenge this presents for high-speed Internet access. Another is the impact of cost on Internet usage where the difference is great between access to a mobile network and a local call on a fixed network. This is why high mobile penetration rates for voice services need to be carefully analysed in relation to short-term Internet developments. In some countries with high mobile penetration rates, most "subscribers" use prepaid cards. These have proved extremely popular with budget-conscious users for many reasons (OECD, 2000h). However, they also are among the most expensive ways to make telephone calls. The structure and pricing levels of prepaid cards would have to change radically before they become "Internet friendly" (OECD, 2000g).

In general, the major factor affecting the formation of a mass of users large enough to create sufficient demand pull for other ICT products and services is the level, and structure, of pricing for Internet access (OECD, 2000g). This is true regardless of the access device used. Those countries that are above the OECD average in Internet penetration are also those that are characterised by unmetered local telecommunication charges (show in quadrant one in Figure 29). This is not the whole story, however. While low access cost stimulates demand, US infrastructure providers also appear better able to respond to new demand rapidly. Infrastructure competition plays a key role in this respect. This suggests that changes in pricing policies, designed to stimulate demand, need to be accompanied by policies that increase competition in areas such as leased lines and backbone networks.

For businesses, the availability and pricing of leased lines are crucial to a supply of electronic commerce services and products. An OECD study on the cost of leased lines provides an overview of capacity and pricing trends for the most commonly used infrastructure for business-to-business electronic commerce (OECD, 2000g). As traffic and capacity sales increase at an unprecedented rate, competition is beginning to arise, and markets for buying and selling capacity are undergoing radical changes. For example, the price of a 2 Mbit/s link between Paris and London at Band-X, a new online bandwidth trading market, plunged almost a third between October 1998 and February 1999 owing to the emergence of new competitive networks.

Figure 29. **Internet host and secure server penetration**

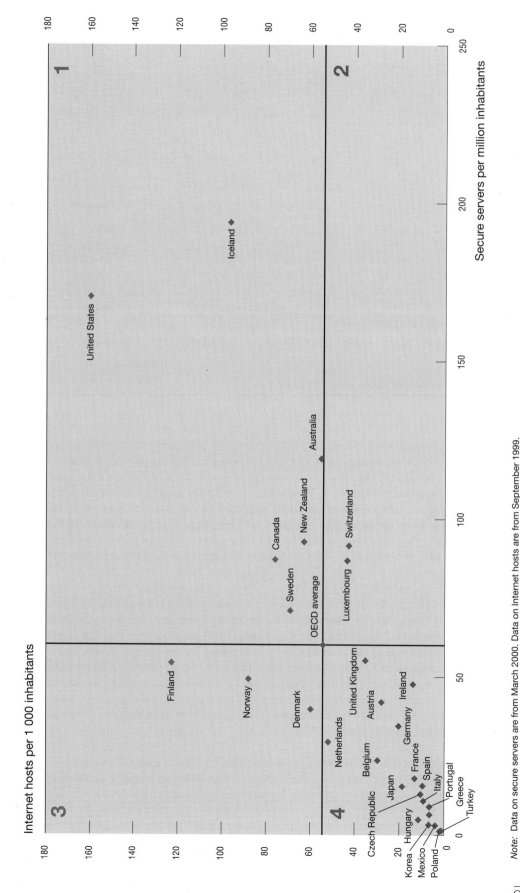

Note: Data on secure servers are from March 2000. Data on Internet hosts are from September 1999.
Group 1 includes countries characterised by unmetered local telecommunication charges (Australia, Canada, New Zealand and the United States) or by relatively inexpensive metered telecommunication access charges to their ISPs (Iceland and Sweden). Groups 2 and 3 include countries with relatively inexpensive Internet access prices and metered telecommunication access to their ISP. They are below the OECD average on Internet host penetration or on secure servers per capita. Group 4 includes all other OECD countries. All countries in Group 4, except Mexico, have metered local telecommunication charges for users to access the Internet, although some of them are now introducing unmetered access charges.
Source: OECD (www.oecd.org/dsti/sti/it/cm) based on Telcordia Technologies (www.netsizer.com) and Netcraft (www.netcraft.com).

Figure 30. **Average price of 20 hours of Internet access and Internet host penetration**

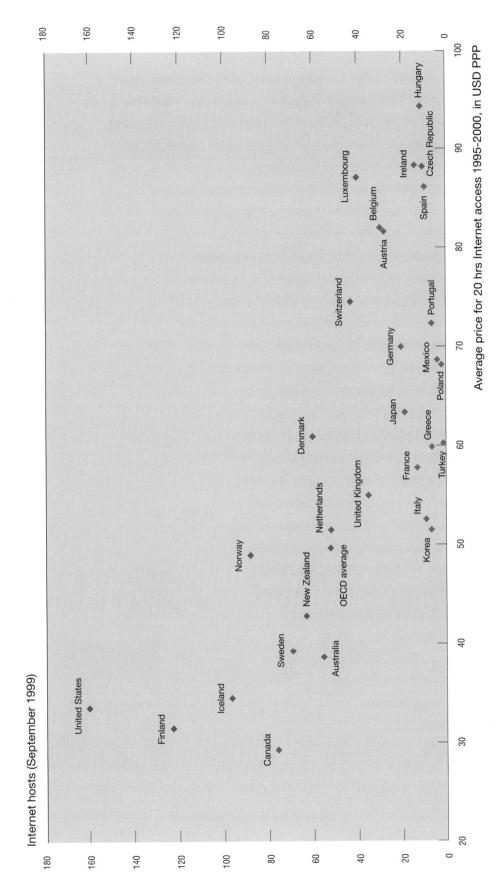

Note: Data on hosts for Luxembourg are from mid-1999. Internet access costs include VAT.
Source: OECD (www.oecd.org/dsti/sti/it/cm) and Telcordia Technologies (www.netsizer.com).

Figure 31. **Tax rate on the consumption of local telecommunication services, 1990-99**

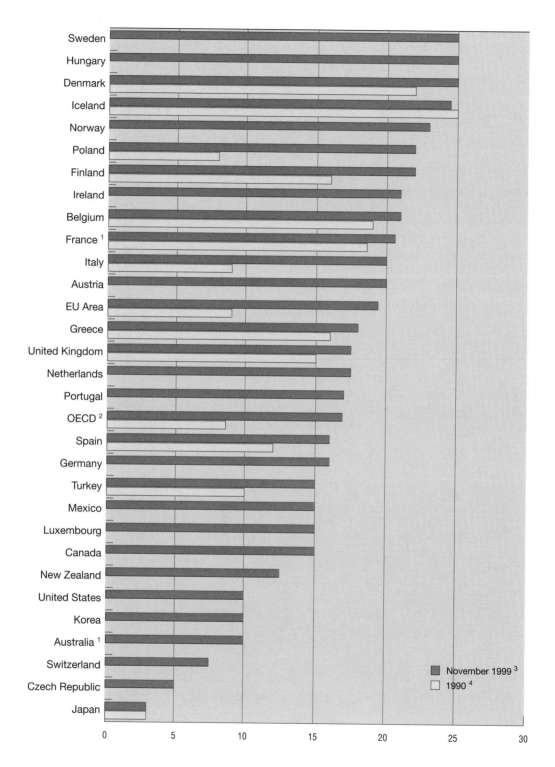

1. France reduced VAT by 1% on 1 April 2000. The rate is now 19.6%. The average excludes this.
2. Average of available countries.
3. November 1999 includes July 2000 data for Australia.
4. Most OECD countries had no taxes on local communications services in 1990.
Source: OECD (2000g).

Nevertheless, the average intra-European price for a 2 Mbit/second leased line in February 1999 was six times higher than the intra-North American price (USD 13 vs. USD 2) (OECD, 1999j).

For households and small businesses, the main cost factor is local telephone access charges. These charges typically represent two-thirds of the costs of accessing the Internet for 20 hours at off-peak times (Figure 30). In recent years, telecommunication charges have been undergoing a process known as "rebalancing", which has involved a lowering of "long-distance" charges and a raising of charges for fixed network elements and local calls. While raising fixed charges did not affect countries with unmetered local charges, raising local call charges significantly increased the cost of Internet access for some countries between 1995 and 1998. Since that time, the negative impact of rebalancing has been mitigated to some extent by the increasing separation of the pricing of local telephony and Internet access. However, for the period under consideration, higher local call charges discouraged online use in metered environments. Countries such as Denmark, Finland and Norway have relatively high penetration of Internet hosts but are below average for indicators of electronic commerce development such as secure servers. In these countries, Internet access prices are low but telecommunication charges are metered. The case of Finland, where some telecommunication carriers offered unmetered pricing until the mid-1990s but have since turned to metered pricing, is especially interesting. This change appears to have slowed the development of electronic commerce over the Internet in Finland, as users stay on line, on average, for less time than in countries where unmetered access is available even though access rates are high (OECD, 2000g).

Differences in Internet access pricing are also influenced by consumption taxes. The OECD average tax rate on telecommunication services almost doubled during the 1990s, from 8.6% to 16.8%. This increase seems to contradict the stated policies of many countries to broaden access to, and encourage usage of, the Internet (Figure 31). Countries with metered access have, on average, a tax rate 5% higher than those with unmetered prices. However, differences generated by metered and unmetered pricing structures make an even greater impact on Internet access. Not only do the users in countries with metered access pay a higher tax rate, they also pay significantly more as their online time increases (OECD, 2000g). For 20 off-peak hours of Internet access, taxes represent about 5% of the total cost in Japan, 10% in the United States[31] and 19% in the European Union.

Chapter 4

POLICIES THAT SUPPORT GROWTH BASED ON INNOVATION AND INFORMATION TECHNOLOGY

Links between policy and economic performance

The previous two chapters suggest that a new wave of innovation, primarily based on information and communication technologies (ICT), is surging through OECD economies. This is true whether or not one agrees that some OECD economies have moved to a "new economy", a "knowledge-based economy" or an "information economy". Rather, the pick-up in multi-factor productivity (MFP) growth in some OECD countries, the important and growing impact of ICT capital and the continuing importance of high-skilled labour all point to the important role played by innovation and technological change in the recent growth performance of OECD economies, particularly the United States.

The previous chapters also suggest that there have been significant changes in the drivers of innovation and in the role of innovation in economic growth. Information technology, in particular, has already had a substantial impact on growth and may offer the possibility of improved performance throughout the economy, even in sectors previously characterised by slow productivity growth and a low degree of innovation. While the potential is there, current growth in OECD countries suggests that only a few countries, and particularly the United States, have been able to reap the benefits of information technology and other developments in the area of innovation. This suggests that the benefits of technological change are conditional on a range of complementary factors and policies. The examination in Chapters 2 and 3 of the factors and policies that help support innovation and the investment and diffusion of ICT indicates that there is no silver bullet for improving growth performance. The present analysis, while preliminary, points to a number of apparently important factors. These are by no means the only ones that affect growth performance, but they are considered of special importance in promoting greater innovation and technological change.

- *Competition matters*. Firms will only invest in efficiency-enhancing technology and in innovation if competition and regulatory reform force them to do so. Competition is also important for lowering costs, a key factor in the diffusion of technologies such as ICT and the Internet. By and large, many of the successful countries identified in Chapter 1 of this report – Australia, Denmark, Ireland, the Netherlands and the United States – have gone through a long process of structural reform aimed at promoting regulatory reform and greater competition.

- *Investment in ICT is making an important contribution to growth and labour productivity growth across the OECD*. However, OECD countries differ in their take-up of ICT, partly owing to the late or slow liberalisation of telecommunications markets in many countries. This has limited investment in the necessary infrastructure and raised costs. Many successful OECD countries moved early to liberalise the telecommunications industry.

- *There is evidence that the Internet and electronic commerce can make a substantial contribution to economic growth, particularly in service industries*. The take-up of the Internet differs considerably across OECD countries. Canada, the Nordic countries and the United States are leaders in terms of Internet host

73

density. Regulatory frameworks, pricing of local calls, and a low critical mass of ICT users in some countries help to explain cross-country differences in Internet use.

- **Networking and openness are of growing importance for innovation.** Knowledge has a wider variety of sources and innovation requires a broader range of technologies and ideas so that there is a greater need for co-operation. Important elements include the ability to establish technology alliances and to engage in mergers and acquisitions, as well as openness to trade and foreign direct investment. While co-operation in pre-competitive research appears required, it needs to be balanced against a strong role for competition authorities at later states.

- **Innovation in emerging areas requires favourable conditions for start-up firms.** In emerging areas, where demand patterns are unclear, risks are large and the technology has not yet been worked out, such firms may have an advantage over large established firms. Differences in the conditions for start-ups, such as their access to venture capital and the degree to which they are subject to administrative regulations, may affect innovation and economic performance. Many "successful" OECD economies, including Australia, Denmark, Ireland and the United States, have relatively low administrative barriers for start-ups.

- **Differences in financial systems, particularly the degree to which they are able to finance risky projects, may affect innovation in emerging industries such as ICT.** Countries with well-developed financial markets and active venture capitalists, such as Canada, the Netherlands, the United Kingdom and the United States, may be better geared towards innovation and the reallocation of capital to new industries than countries such as Germany and Japan where traditional banking plays a dominant role. There is no evidence to suggest that countries with bank-based systems should move to a system based on financial markets, but the presence of aspects of both systems may be a source of robustness.

- **Innovation in areas such as ICT and biotechnology draws increasingly and more directly on scientific progress.** Links between science and industry are not equally developed across OECD countries. While reform is under way in many countries, regulatory frameworks and deficient incentive structures continue to limit co-operation. The United States has been the first to engage in reform in this area, with notable impacts on innovative performance. Several successful countries, including Denmark, Finland and the United States, seem to have strong links between science and industrial innovation.

- **Public support for basic scientific research remains important to increase the stock of fundamental knowledge and to provide highly skilled graduates.** Scientific institutions are also important for technology diffusion and innovation, and are of increasing importance for countries that want to benefit from the global stock of knowledge.

- **Human capital is a key factor in the innovation process, and many innovation surveys suggest that the lack of skilled personnel is a principal barrier to innovation.** Education policies and frameworks for lifelong learning appear important. Some countries have benefited substantially from the immigration of highly skilled personnel, Australia and the United States being the clearest examples. While a case can be made for greater international mobility of human resources, countries will also need to address skills and education at the domestic level.

Strong economic performance does not depend on any one of these factors alone, but requires the combination of these – and other – factors. They include stable and supportive macroeconomic policies; significant liberalisation of product markets over the past two decades, for instance in transport, finance and communications; trade liberalisation; flexible labour markets; and a strong entrepreneurial climate. This combination is most clearly present in the United States but is – at this time – only in evidence to some extent in other OECD countries. The special character of US economic growth is confirmed in other studies. Recent studies point to a number of factors that have helped to improve innovation and growth performance (National Research Council, 1999a, 1999b; Scarpetta et al., 2000). Some US policies have also been of special importance in strengthening innovation. A series of legislative changes in the 1980s enabled collaboration in pre-competitive research and helped the business sector to achieve the necessary restructuring. Changes in patent legislation, starting with the 1980 Bayh-Dole Act which extended patent protection to publicly funded research, have had a significant impact on the rate of technology transfer from the public sector. Also underlying strong US performance are the important scientific and technological breakthroughs that have emerged from publicly funded research over the past decades. Many key technologies, such as graphical interfaces and the Internet, have emerged from publicly funded research. Support for the research infrastructure in this area, *e.g.* high-capacity networks, has also been important (National Research Council, 1998). These changes in the policy framework and growing pressures due to globalisation have significantly changed how US firms operate. Firms have specialised, focusing on core competencies and outsourcing many other activities, have consolidated their activities and have focused more on internationalisation. Most importantly, however, the US business sector has shown a greater ability to introduce new products and processes, often from new firms.

Evidence for countries such as Australia, Denmark and the Netherlands attributes their strong economic performance primarily to a long process of structural reform. All of these countries have followed many of the recommendations of the OECD Jobs Strategy (OECD 1998a; OECD, 1999g). In most, new factors of particular importance to the emergence of new growth industries such as ICT and biotechnology seem to play a limited role at this stage. However, the process of structural reform is most likely a necessary requirement before effective use of ICT and greater innovation can take hold in the economy. In this respect, these economies may be quite well placed to capture the potential benefits of ICT and innovation in the future.

Country-specific evidence supports the idea that structural reform has played an important role in several countries. A recent study for Australia links the significant improvement in MFP growth over the past decade to a range of microeconomic reforms (Productivity Commission, 1999). These reforms have helped to improve the allocation of resources, enhanced specialisation, encouraged reorganisation and the implementation of better work and management practices, increased the use of advanced technologies and the rate of innovation and raised workforce skills. Growth performance in the Irish economy can also be attributed to a range of structural factors, with the ability to attract FDI the basis for much of Ireland's success (OECD, 1999k). In Denmark and the Netherlands, improved growth performance can be linked to structural reforms in both product and labour markets (OECD, 1999g). In the Netherlands, however, improved growth performance has not been accompanied by faster MFP growth, mainly because growth has brought many low-skilled workers back into the labour force, thus lowering the rate of productivity growth (Pomp, 1998).

Most other OECD countries that have improved performance over the past decade are significantly smaller than the United States and some of the drivers of performance are different (OECD, 1999b). Large and highly developed countries, such as the United States, offer markets with advanced customers and opportunities to reap economies of scale while maintaining diversity in R&D activities. Innovators in smaller, high-income countries generally have to internationalise more rapidly and specialise more narrowly to reap these benefits (*e.g.* mobile communications in Finland). Free flows of technology across borders are important to these countries, and their innovation systems often focus on capturing the benefits of technology inflows. The strong performance of some small countries is confirmed by the empirical evidence, which indicates a strong negative correlation between the size of OECD countries and their GDP growth rate.[32] It may be that medium-sized countries have not yet sufficiently adapted to the greater need for openness in their economies. This issue merits further research, however, since some large economies have also suffered important macroeconomic shocks.

Policies to promote innovation and technological change

Establishing a favourable climate for business

The previous section noted the importance of structural reform in bringing out the benefits of innovation and technological progress. Competition is of particular importance. Firms will invest in innovation if they can expect sufficient private returns and if competition forces them to improve performance. OECD work has shown that regulatory reform, if it leads to stronger competition, can enhance productivity, reduce costs and strengthen innovation (OECD, 1997c). Greater competition is particularly important for driving down the costs of ICT, telecommunications and the Internet; this is a necessity in a society where low-cost access to and diffusion of these technologies is important for business performance and innovation.[33]

Other important factors also affect the business climate, however, and have been discussed in previous OECD studies. They include flexible labour markets, well-functioning product and financial markets, and favourable conditions for entrepreneurship. Rules that unduly limit the establishment of a new firm or excessively penalise an exiting firm may also deter innovation and economic restructuring.

New types of financing and improved risk management

New financing mechanisms, such as venture capital and secondary stock markets, are important in funding new firms and risky ventures and in overcoming the information problems associated with them. The analysis of financial markets and their general impact on economic growth is a complex area requiring further work.[34] Nevertheless, it is possible to make a few observations about the interaction of finance and innovation in the 1990s. First, equity markets may be a better source of finance than traditional forms of debt for new innovative firms, given their often limited cash flow, absence of collateral and high risk (the upside of which does not benefit lenders). Financial markets may also be better geared towards the necessary economic restructuring that accompanies the emergence of technologies with economy-wide applications, such as ICT (Tsuru, 2000).

New forms of financing high-risk innovation, such as venture capital, are important to support activities that lack assets and need to be nurtured by experienced managers. While public policies can play a role in helping to establish these funds, the creation of a wider set of favourable conditions may be more important. First, venture capitalists need to be able to recover their liquidity through an active initial public offerings market or mergers and acquisitions. Second, venture capital firms often need to offer stock options to attract and retain key personnel. Third, new sources of finance for venture capital may be available if institutional investors, such as pension funds, are able to invest some of their funds in risky ventures.

Funding for science and high-risk research

Funding for science and high-risk research remains a core task of governments. A large number of scientific discoveries and inventions occur by chance, sometimes as the by-product of more focused research efforts, but often as the result of scientific curiosity. Such discoveries, which are commonly referred to as serendipity, are, by their nature, unpredictable. The importance of serendipity implies that governments should not go too far in orienting scientific research towards precise economic or social goals. However, governments may be able to give broad directions for long-term research in areas requiring greater understanding. Such funding should be competitive, however, and the prime criteria should be scientific excellence and intellectual merit (Branscomb, 1999).[35]

It is particularly important for government-funded research to continue to provide the early seeds of innovation. The shortening of private-sector product and R&D cycles carries the risk of under-investment in scientific research, generic technologies and other long-term technologies with broad applications (NIST, 1999). In addition, too much commercialisation of publicly funded research carried out in universities and public laboratories will reduce the necessary attention to long-term research. Where government research is needed to meet public goals, such as health, energy and defence, government policy will need to strike a balance between promoting competition for funding versus earmarking funds for specific projects.

Governments, particularly of small OECD countries, cannot fund all fields of science. A growing number of OECD countries therefore complement institutional funding of scientific research with more focused efforts to build capacity. Many of these efforts are aimed at the creation of "centres of excellence", particularly in new fields.[36] Aside from the direct creation of innovation, the creation of world class research centres plays an important role in the formation of research networks and clusters. They help establish a collaborative environment between industry and university researchers and provide a critical mass of people who can extend research further and diffuse the resulting technology. Such centres also act as magnets for highly skilled people from all over the world.

Government support for science and innovation extends beyond support for science and long-term research. Most OECD governments stimulate R&D and innovation in the private sector, as the gap between private and social returns to R&D may mean that the private sector invests too little in R&D and because uncertainty is inherent to innovation. A key question regarding such financial support is whether governments can identify, with sufficient accuracy, the areas to which support should be directed. The issue is not so much "picking winners" as the identification of potential innovations with large externalities (Stiglitz, 1999). Furthermore, the design of such programmes is important, particularly to avoid market distortions. In providing direct support for business R&D, governments will increasingly need to consider whether new sources of finance, such as venture capital, cannot substitute for some of this support.

Policies to strengthen co-operation and encourage diffusion

While policies directed towards the development of technology and innovation are important, so are policies that encourage the diffusion of technology throughout the economy. In addition, the innovation system itself increasingly depends on a sufficient degree of interaction among firms, universities, research institutes and regulators. Competition represents a key policy area for promoting diffusion. The evidence presented in Chapter 3 on the diffusion of the Internet clearly shows that Internet penetration is highest in the countries with the lowest Internet access costs. Access costs seem to reflect the state of competition in telecommunications and the pricing of local calls, including the taxes levied on telecommunications. The OECD-wide trend over the past years towards higher tax rates on telecommunications appears to contradict the need for broader Internet access and lower costs.

Another important area for government policy is the reform of regulations that govern science-industry relationships. Regulatory reform in the United States in the early 1980s, such as the Bayh-Dole Act, have significantly increased the contribution of scientific institutions to innovation. There is evidence that this is one of the factors contributing to the pick-up of US growth performance (Jaffe, 1999; Jaffe and Lerner, 1999). In this area, most OECD countries are in various stages of reform. While the trend towards relaxing regulatory constraints is clear, several other barriers affect the circulation of knowledge between science and industry. First, regulations that affect mobility are important, *e.g.* lack of transferable pension rights between the public and private sector. Second, evaluation and promotion practices in public research often reduce researchers' incentives to co-operate with the business sector or to engage in academic entrepreneurship. While there are good reasons for promoting greater interaction between science and industry, there are also dangers inherent in excessive commercialisation of university research, and appropriate policies in this area require further investigation.[37]

In some cases, legal changes may be required to enable the formation of technology alliances between firms for conducting co-operative pre-competitive research. Such changes should be closely co-ordinated with competition authorities, however, to ensure that they do not compromise competition and with it the incentives to innovate.[38]

Networking and diffusion are not limited by national borders and increasingly require openness and co-operation at global level. Policies directed towards national champions and self-sufficiency in science and technology seem increasingly misguided, as the knowledge required for technological change may come from many sources. Openness of research efforts and the domestic economy to international competition and international knowledge therefore seems of increasing value for promoting diffusion and innovation.

Human capital to support innovation and technological change

Human capital is obviously a key policy area, as it is required for innovation and growth. In addition, citizens need to be able to adapt to a rapidly changing society. Government's role in providing certain types of education and training is important, but individuals and firms have their own role in training and must invest in it themselves. Human capital policies primarily focus on increasing the overall average skill level of the labour force, as this is important for facilitating the adoption and use of technologies. Frameworks for lifelong learning appear of particular importance during the current rapid technological change which is likely to require new skills. However, there is also a growing need for highly skilled individuals, *e.g.* in the science system and the ICT sector.

Three policy areas merit further attention in this respect. First, several OECD Member countries have benefited from the immigration of skilled foreign workers, while others have been affected by a "brain drain". Further analysis may be needed to examine how the international mobility of highly skilled personnel affects growth and if and how it can be made more than a zero-sum game. Second, there are concerns in several OECD countries about (future) shortages of scientists and other highly skilled workers. Third, the skills needed in a "new economy" may be very different from those currently available. For instance, creativity and teamwork are likely to become more important. Further analysis of the appropriate policies in these areas seems warranted.

Enhancing the benefits of investment in ICT

Chapter 3 demonstrated the importance of ICT to economic performance. To benefit from investment in ICT, certain complementary policies are essential. The first, and possible most important, factor concerns the regulatory framework and the degree of competition in the telecommunications sector. The evidence clearly shows that investment in ICT is closely linked to the rapid fall in the costs of ICT, and that the diffusion of ICT is closely linked to access costs and the prevailing state of competition. Regulatory reform of the telecommunications sector should lead to more entrants, lower costs, greater diffusion and a higher rate of innovation. The need for competition extends beyond the telecommunications sector, however, to the provision of ICT equipment and services.

Competition in the local telecommunications loop is of particular importance in this respect. The absence of competition in the local loop enables dominant operators to disregard the changing needs of businesses and users in relation to electronic commerce. Government intervention to impose tariffs more favourable to electronic commerce runs counter to the principle of allowing telecommunication carriers to manage tariff structures and should be avoided. Moreover, it has become clear that, for consumers and small businesses, the structure of pricing is at least as important as its absolute level. Policies encouraging the deployment of high-speed Internet access options hold tremendous promise for improving Internet access. However, relying on the development of high-speed infrastructure, without provision for competition, may not expand access to electronic commerce.

A firm's effective use of ICT typically requires organisational change, restructuring and investment in human capital. While some of these are beyond the scope of government policy, governments can create an environment that is supportive of such change. It would entail the ability of firms to restructure without undue restrictions, flexible labour markets, ease of entry and exit in particular markets and measures that facilitate the mobility of personnel.

As ICT transforms the economy, it will also be important to ensure that regulations do not limit the creation of new products and services based on ICT which extend beyond traditional sectoral boundaries (*e.g.* software firms offering financial services). Governments may lead the way in creating the critical mass for ICT, *e.g.* by offering public services on line and procuring government needs on line.

Some final considerations

While innovation and technological change appear of great importance for strengthening growth performance, they may also have undesirable effects. There are concerns that the rapid spread of information technology may lead to a "digital divide" between those with access to the technology and those without. This might further reinforce the skill bias of technological change and increase the gap in opportunities between low-skilled and high-skilled workers. In addition, some OECD countries are concerned that the financial benefits from innovation may accrue only to a small proportion of the population and increase earnings inequalities. Some of the social changes linked to a "new economy" may also not be well captured by conventional statistics. It is unclear to what extent these effects are significant, since the recent US experience suggests a decline in income inequality and higher employment rates for low-skilled workers. It is also true that many of these effects are not new. Rapid technological change has often been accompanied by major social changes, and policy makers can help best by providing people with the tools and skills that enable them to adjust to these changes. Lifelong learning is one of those tools.

The argument has also been made that some countries and cultures may be better able to adapt to rapid growth and innovation than others. Cultural attitudes may, for instance, affect the willingness of people to take risks, to start a firm or to migrate (OECD, 1999l) and also affect a country's institutional framework. Both cultural and institutional factors may thus affect the transferability of some policies and policy instruments across OECD countries. The US experience may therefore be of limited relevance to some other OECD countries. However, culture is not a static thing, and attitudes towards risk and entrepreneurship may be modified, for instance, by changes in taxation, regulations, labour markets and the education system. Issues such as trust and the basic confidence in society are also important in this respect and are the topic on ongoing work in the OECD.

It is also clear that ICT and innovation are changing OECD economies and societies in ways that are still only partly understood. For instance, it is claimed that ICT may lead to better-functioning product and factor markets, by increasing transparency and promoting international competition. There are also some indications that ICT may facilitate the innovation process. Further analysis will be required in these areas to collect evidence, understand these processes and respond with appropriate policy frameworks.

When designing policies directed towards a more innovative economy, certain factors should be taken into account. First, policy change takes time, and its effects may then take some time to appear. The recent success of countries such as Australia and the Netherlands seems linked to structural reforms in labour and product markets that occurred over a long period in the 1980s and 1990s. Much of the US success is built on changes to the framework of the economy in the 1980s. Efforts to create a more innovative economy, for instance by appropriate investment in science and ICT, may also take time to become effective.

Second, it is clear from the above that improving growth performance depends on many factors and policies. There is no silver bullet for addressing growth disparities in the OECD area. The experience of several successful OECD economies shows that only a broad and co-ordinated package of policies can strengthen growth. This package includes stable and supportive macroeconomic policies, structural reform in labour, product and financial markets, improved conditions for business and entrepreneurship, sufficient investment in human capital, innovation and science and a sufficient degree of competition. The available evidence suggests that countries may be unlikely to reap the potential benefits from ICT and greater innovation unless this broader framework in place. Wiring schools will not be enough.

NOTES

1. The role of ICT in capital deepening largely reflects technical change. What is treated as a quantitative change in ICT investment actually reflects price adjustments for qualitative changes in ICT capital.

2. Innovation relates to the introduction of new products, processes and organisational structures. It differs from technological change, since it also includes non-technological changes, and since technological change incorporates the diffusion of existing technologies. A definition of innovation is provided in OECD's *Oslo Manual* (OECD, 1997a).

3. The role of R&D in MFP growth will be further examined in the second phase of the OECD work.

4. Innovation surveys suggest that the non-R&D portion of firms' expenditure on innovation is up to twice the R&D portion (OECD, 1999b).

5. There may be a considerable time lag between investment and innovation, however.

6. Not all innovations are patented, making them difficult to quantify. Some are protected by copyright and trademark, while others are protected by secrecy or first-to-market strategies.

7. Most innovation in services is not patented. This implies that indicators of innovation in services are often more indicative in nature, *e.g.* investment in innovation.

8. The role of mergers and acquisitions is discussed below.

9. The use of stock options is controversial for several reasons. First, it can lead to very high rewards for executives and employees and thus increase earnings inequalities. Second, options may impede judgements about prospective earnings per share and dilute shareholder value. Third, they imply an assymetric risk structure for executives, which may affect behaviour.

10. These trends are discussed in greater detail in OECD (1998a; 1998b).

11. The data presented in Figure 13 refer to alliances containing arrangements for technology transfer or joint research. The data are drawn from the MERIT-CATI database, which is based on alliances that have been published in the press (Hagedoorn, 1996). The data should therefore be viewed as indicative, rather than comprehensive.

12. An extensive discussion of the role of co-operation can be found in National Science Foundation (1998a).

13. For instance, the US Financial Services Technology Consortium aimed to develop digital images of paper checks to facilitate interbank exchange of such checks.

14. The average number of member companies in these 665 research ventures is about 13 firms (NSF, 1998a).

15. For instance, the growth of mergers and acquisitions in areas such as pharmaceuticals seems closely linked to the growing costs of drug development.

16. High-technology start-ups are only a small proportion of all SMEs. The SME sector is very heterogeneous, with a high degree of churning, due to high entry and exit rates. Empirical studies suggest that high-growth firms can emerge in all areas of the SME segment, but that their growth is often closely linked to technology use and a high degree of innovation.

17. Scientific research is important not only for economic objectives, but also in its own right.

18. In some cases, firms appear to find a large in-house scientific capability a liability rather than an asset, as it reduces flexibility and may create too large a focus on "make" rather than "buy" strategies.

19. Measured here as the intensity of citation of scientific publications in industrial patents.

20. Venture capitalists are a particularly important source of market knowledge, skills and management. See below.

21. For instance, the Russian Internet search engine firm, Yandex, builds on this process. See "Russian Brain Drain Reversed", *Financial Times*, 6 March 2000.

22. See, for example, Triplett (1999) for a review.

23. In line with the 1968 System of National Accounts, software was treated as an intermediate good. Under the new 1993 System of National Accounts, software is treated as an investment good but few countries have implemented this change. Neglecting software implies a substantial underestimation of the role of ICT in capital formation and in its contribution to output. However, if software is treated as an investment rather than an intermediate good, final output will also increase and counterbalance a rise in the share of output generated by ICT capital. Another neglected item is the contribution to growth of labour associated with ICT investment, such as computer services. In this sense, the results of the study constitute a lower rather than an upper bound for the contribution of ICT to output growth.

24. The recent studies apply the latest data that were not yet available to Gordon. These data also incorporate substantial revisions by the Bureau of Economic Analysis. In addition, Gordon's adjustment for the business cycle lowers overall productivity growth, but leaves the percentage point contribution of computers unaffected, thus raising the contribution of computers to overall productivity growth.

25. And vice versa. The growing importance of ICT in the economy is accompanied by a growing demand for ICT-related services. This is one factor that is driving the increasing weight of services in the economy, and one that is closely to the emergence of a knowledge-based economy.

26. Rapid productivity growth in banking can also be observed in Finland, where the combined effects of a banking crisis and the aggressive adoption of ICT forced a restructuring away from traditional branch banks and towards ATMs and Internet banking. A quarter of the adult population now handles the bulk of their banking via the Internet (OECD, 2000f). Consequently, transactions per employee have more than doubled since the early 1990s and cash in circulation as a share of GDP is less than half of the EU average (OECD, 1999h).

27. A study by Abernathy *et al.* (1999) on the US textile and apparel industry shows that improvements in performance depend on the adoption of a combination of ICT technologies along the industry value chain. The number of technological innovations adopted had statistically significant effects on firms' lead times, inventory levels and volatility, as well as profit margins.

28. Goldman Sachs (2000), "GM-Ford-DaimlerChrysler Exchange", 1 March.

29. Non-proprietary (free) standards for the Internet include the transport control protocol/Internet protocol (TCP/IP) and the standard coding system of the World Wide Web, hypertext markup language (HTML).

30. For example, the Internet can offer a manufacturing EDI system at about one-quarter the cost associated with a value-added network over a leased line (Meeker, 1997).

31. Based on New York state sales tax.

32. This excludes the United States. The correlation coefficient was -0.54 over 1991-99 and -0.58 over 1996-99. The strong negative correlation is a significant change from previous decades. In the 1960s, large countries grew faster than small countries.

33. It is important to note that regulatory reform is not only important for product markets, but increasingly also affects other areas of public-private interactions, *e.g.* education and scientific research.

34. Work on financial markets is currently under way in the OECD for the final report to Ministers in 2001.

35. A project on the funding of basic research is currently under way at the OECD.

36. For example, the US Department of Defence's Defence Advanced Research Projects Agency (DARPA) provided federal funding that established computer science and software engineering in US universities such as MIT, University of California at Berkeley, Stanford and Carnegie Mellon. Federal support has constituted about 70% of total university research funding in computer science and engineering since 1976 (National Research Council, 1999b).

37. Work on science-industry relationships is currently under way in the OECD.

38. This is also an area where further investigation is warranted in the second stage of the OECD work on growth.

OECD 2000

BIBLIOGRAPHY

ABERNATHY, F.H., J. DUNLOP, J.H. HAMMOND and D. WEIL (1999), A *Stitch in Time*, Oxford University Press.

ANCHORDOGUY, M. (2000), "Japan's Software Industry: A Failure of Institutions?", *Research Policy*, No. 29.

AUSTRIAN FEDERAL MINISTRY FOR ECONOMIC AFFAIRS (1998), *Business Services and Employment*, Vienna.

BASSANINI, A., S. SCARPETTA and I. VISCO (2000), "Knowledge, Technology and Economic Growth: Recent Evidence from OECD Countries", paper prepared for the 150th Anniversary Conference of the National Bank of Belgium, Brussels, May.

BEBCHUK, L. (1999), "A Rent-Protection Theory of Corporate Ownership and Control", *Harvard Law School Discussion Paper*, No. 260.

BLACK, S.E. and L.M. LYNCH (1997), "How to Compete: The Impact of Workplace Practices and Information Technology on Productivity", NBER *Working Paper*, No. 6120, August.

BLACK, S.E. and L.M. LYNCH (2000), "What's Driving the New Economy? The Benefits of Workplace Innovation", NBER *Working Paper*, No. 7479, January.

BLONDAL, S. and D. PILAT (1997), "The Economic Benefits of Regulatory Reform", OECD *Economic Studies*, No. 28, 1997/I, pp. 7-48.

BRANSCOMB, L.M. (1999), "The False Dichotomy: Scientific Creativity and Utility", *Issues in Science and Technology*, Fall.

BRESNAHAN, T.F (1999), "Computing", in National Research Council, U.S. *Industry in 2000 - Studies in Competitive Performance*, National Academy Press, Washington, DC.

BRESNAHAN, T.F., E. BRYNJOLFSSON and L. HITT (1999), "Information Technology, Workplace Organisation, and the Demand for Skilled Labor: Firm-level Evidence", NBER *Working Paper*, No. 7136, May.

BROERSMA, L. and R.H. McGUCKIN (1999), "The Impact of Computers on Productivity in the Trade Sector: Explorations with Dutch Microdata", *Research Memorandum* GD-45, Groningen Growth and Development Centre, October.

BROUWER, E. and A. KLEINKNECHT (1999), "Innovative Output and a Firm's Propensity to Patent. An Exploration of CIS Micro Data", *Research Policy*, Vol. 28, pp. 615-624.

BRYNJOLFSSON, E. and C. KEMERER (1996), "Network Externalities in Microcomputer Software: An Econometric Analysis of the Spreadsheet Market", *Management Science*, Vol. 42, pp. 1627-1647.

BRYNJOLFSSON, E. and L. HITT (1997), "Computing Productivity: Are Computers Pulling Their Weight?", mimeo, MIT and Wharton, http://ccs.mit.edu/erik/cpg/.

BRYNJOLFSSON, E., L. HITT and S. YANG (1998), "Intangible Assets: How the Interaction of Information Systems and Organisational Structure Affects Stock Market Valuations", forthcoming in *Proceedings of the International Conference on Information Systems*, Helsinki, Finland.

BRYNJOLFSSON, E. and S. YANG (1998), "The Intangible Benefits and Costs of Computer Investments: Evidence from the Financial Markets", mimeo, May, http://ccs.mit.edu/erik/.

BUREAU OF ECONOMIC ANALYSIS (BEA) (2000), "Selected NIPA Tables", www.bea.doc.gov, Washington, DC.

CAMERON, G. (1998), "Innovation and Growth: A Survey of the Empirical Evidence", Nuffield College, Oxford, July, http://hicks.nuff.ox.ac.uk/users/cameron/research/gpapers.html#P3.

CARLIN, W. and C. MAYER (1999), "Finance, Investment and Growth", in L. Renneboog and J. McCahery (eds.), *Convergence and Diversity in Corporate Governance Regimes and Capital Markets*, Cambridge University Press, Cambridge.

CARRINGTON, W.J. and E. DETRAGIACHE (1998), "How Big is the Brain Drain?", *International Monetary Fund Working Paper*, No. 102, July.

CHAKRABORTY, A. and M. KAZAROSIAN (1999), "Product Differentiation and the Use of Information Technology: New Evidence from the Trucking Industry", NBER *Working Paper*, No. 7222, July.

COUNCIL OF ECONOMIC ADVISORS (2000), *Economic Report of the President*, US Government Printing Office.

CPB NETHERLANDS BUREAU FOR ECONOMIC POLICY ANALYSIS (2000), *Central Economic Plan 2000*, The Hague.

DARBY, M.R. and L.G. ZUCKER (1999a), "Local Academic Science Driving Organizational Change: The Adoption of Biotechnology by Japanese Firms", NBER *Working Paper*, No. 7248, July.

DARBY, M.R., Q. LIU and L.G. ZUCKER (1999b), "Stakes and Stars: The Effect of Intellectual Human Capital on the Level and Variability of High-tech Firms' Market Values", NBER *Working Paper*, No. 7201, June.

DATAMONITOR (1999), *Business-to-business Electronic Commerce*, London.

DAVIS, B. (1998), "In Certificates We Trust", http://www.techweb.com, 25 March.

DEN HERTOG, P. and R. BILDERBEEK (1998), *The New Knowledge Infrastructure: The Role of Technology-Based Knowledge-Intensive Business Services in National Innovation Systems*, SI4S Project, STEP Group, Oslo.

DEPARTMENT OF TRADE AND INDUSTRY (1999), UK *Competitiveness Indicators 1999*, London.

DESMET, D., T. FRANCIS, A. HU, T.M. KOLLER and G.A. RIEDEL (2000), "Valuing dot-coms", *The McKinsey Quarterly*, 2000, No. 1, McKinsey & Company.

DHUME, S. (2000), "Bringing It Home", *Far Eastern Economic Review*, 17 February.

ELECTRONIC COMMERCE PROMOTION COUNCIL OF JAPAN (ECOM) (1999), *Survey and Analysis of the Economic Impact of EC on the Japanese Economy*, March.

EUROPEAN PRIVATE EQUITY AND VENTURE CAPITAL ASSOCIATION (EVCA) (1999), *1999 Yearbook*, Brussels.

FAGERBERG, J. (1994), "Technology and International Differences in Growth Rates", *Journal of Economic Literature*, Vol. 32, September, pp. 1147-1175.

FIXLER, D. and K. ZIESCHANG (1999), "The Productivity of the Banking Sector: Integrating Approaches to Measuring Financial Service Output", *Canadian Journal of Economics*, Vol. 32.

FOSGERAU, M. and A. SORESEN (1999), "Deflation and Decomposition of Danish Value-added Growth using the KLEMS Methodology", paper prepared for the Workshop on International Comparisons of Productivity, organised by CEBR, Ministry of Trade and Industry, Denmark, 10 December.

FRANK, R.D., E.R. BERNDT and S.H. BUSCH (1998), "Price Indexes for the Treatment of Depression", NBER *Working Paper*, No. W6417.

GANDAL, N., S. GREENSTEIN and D. SALANT (1999), "Adoptions and Orphans in the Early Microcomputer Market", *Journal of Industrial Economics*, Vol. 47, pp. 97-116.

GERA, S., W. GU and F.C. LEE (1999), "Information Technology and Labour Productivity Growth: An Empirical Analysis for Canada and the United States", *Canadian Journal of Economics*, Vol. 32, No. 2, pp. 384-407.

GIRISHANKAR, S. (1997b), "Feds Get Down to Business with Latest E-commerce Push", http://www.techweb.com, 3 November.

GOKHBERG, L., N. KOVALEVA, L. MINDEI and E. NEKIPELOVA (2000), *Qualified Manpower in Russia*, Centre for Scientific Research and Statistics, Moscow.

GOLDMAN SACHS US (1999), "B2B: 2B or Not 2B?", E-commerce/Internet, Goldman Sachs Investment Research, 14 September.

GORDON, R.J. (1999), "Has the 'New Economy' Rendered the Productivity Slowdown Obsolete?", Northwestern University and NBER, mimeo.

GRIFFITH, R., S. REDDING and J. VAN REENEN (1998), "Productivity Growth in OECD Industries: Identifying the Role of R&D, Skills and Trade", Institute for Fiscal Studies, London, mimeo.

GU, W. and M. HO (2000), "A Comparison of Productivity Growth in Manufacturing between Canada and the United States, 1961-1995", paper presented at the CSLS Conference on the Canada-US Manufacturing Productivity Gap, 21-22 January, Ottawa, Ontario.

HAGEDOORN, J. (1996), "Trends and Patterns in Strategic Technology Partnering Since the Early Seventies", *Review of Industrial Organization*, Vol. 11, No. 5, pp. 601-616.

HALL, B.H. (1999), "Innovation and Market Value", NBER *Working Paper*, No. 6984, February.

HAUSMAN, J. (1997), "Cellular Telephone, New Products and the CPI", NBER *Working Paper*, No. 5982.

HICKS, D and J. S. KATZ (1997) "The Changing Shape of British Industrial Research", STEP *Special Report*, No. 6, STEP Group, Oslo.

HITT, L. and E. BRYNJOLFSSON (1997), "Information Technology and Internal Firm Organisation: An Exploratory Analysis", *Journal of Management Information Systems*, Vol. 14(2).

HITT, L.M. and E. BRYNJOLFSSON (1998), "Beyond Computation: Information Technology, Organisational Transformation and Business Performance", http://ccs.mit.edu/erik/, mimeo.

IANSITI, M. and J. WEST (1997), "Technology Integration: Turning Great Research into Great Products", *Harvard Business Review*, May-June, pp. 69-79.

INTERNATIONAL DATA CORPORATION (IDC) (1999), "Internet Insights, 1999", *The Grey Sheet*, Vol. 33, Nos. 21-22, March 23.

JAFFE, A.B. (1999), "The U.S. Patent System in Transition: Policy Innovation and the Innovation Process", NBER *Working Paper*, No. 7280, Cambridge, MA.

JAFFE, A.B. and J. LERNER (1999), "Privatizing R&D: Patent Policy and the Commercialization of National Laboratory Technologies", NBER *Working Paper*, No. 7064, April.

JORGENSON, D.W. and K.J. STIROH (2000), "Raising the Speed Limit: U.S. Economic Growth in the Information Age", Harvard University and Federal Reserve Bank of New York, March 3, mimeo.

KANG, N-H and S. JOHANSSON (2000), "Cross-Border Mergers and Acquisitions: Their Role in Industrial Globalisation", STI *Working Papers* 2000/1, OECD, Paris.

KATZ, J.S. and D. HICKS (1998), *Indicators for Systems of Innovation*, IDEA Paper 12-1998, STEP Group, Oslo.

KORTUM S. and J. LERNER (1998a), "Stronger Protection or Technological Revolution: What is Behind the Recent Surge in Patenting?", *Carnegie-Rochester Conference Series on Public Policy*, Vol. 48, No. 1, pp. 247-304.

KORTUM, S. and J. LERNER (1998b), "Does Venture Capital Spur Innovation?", NBER *Working Paper*, No. 6846, December.

LARSON, C.F. (1999), "Research in Industry", in *Research and Development* FY 2000, AAAS Report XXIV, American Association for the Advancement for Science, Chapter 4.

LEBOW, D., L. SHEINER, L. SLIFMAN and M. STARR-McCLUER (1999), "Recent Trends in Compensation Practices", *Finance and Economics Discussion Series*, 1999-32, Federal Reserve Board.

LICHTENBERG, F.R. (1995), "The Output Contributions of Computer Equipment and Personal: A Firm Level Analysis", *Economics of Innovation and New Technology*, Vol. 3.

LICHTENBERG, F. and B. VAN POTTELSBERGHE DE LA POTTERIE (2000), "Does Foreign Direct Investment Transfer Technology Across Borders?", Columbia University, mimeo.

LIPSEY, R.G. (1999) "Sources of Continued Long-run Economic Dynamism in the 21st Century", *The Future of the Global Economy*, OECD, Paris.

MAHER, M. and T. ANDERSSON, (1999), "Corporate Governance: Effects on Firm Performance and Economic Growth", in L. Renneboog and J. McCahery (eds.), *Convergence and Diversity in Corporate Governance Regimes and Capital Markets*, Cambridge University Press, Cambridge.

MALONE, T.W. and R.J. LAUBACHER (1998), "The Dawn of the E-Lance Economy", *Harvard Business Review*, September-October.

MANN, C.L. (1997), "Globalisation and Productivity in the United States and Germany", Board of Governors of the Federal Reserve System, *International Finance Discussion Papers*, No. 595, November.

MANN, C. (1999), *Is the US Trade Deficit Sustainable?*, Institute for International Economics, Washington, DC.

MANNHEIM INNOVATION PANEL (1999), *Services in the Future – Innovation Activities in the Services Sector*, Mannheim.

MARGHERIO, L., D. HENRY, S. COOK, and S. MONTES (1998), "The Emerging Digital Economy", US Department of Commerce, Washington, DC, http://www.ecommerce.gov, April.

MCGUCKIN, R.H. and K.J. STIROH, (1998), "Computers Can Accelerate Productivity Growth", *Issues in Science and Technology*, Summer.

MCKELVEY, M. (forthcoming), "Global Forums, Small Countries: Ericsson, Nokia and Wireless Telecommunications", *International Journal of Technology Management*.

MCMILLAN, G.S., F. NARIN and D.L. DEEDS (2000), "An Analysis of the Critical Role of Public Science in Innovation: The Case of Biotechnology", *Research Policy*, Vol. 29, pp.1-8.

MEEKER, M. (1997), "Internet Retailing Report", Morgan Stanley, http://www.ms.com, 28 May.

MINISTRY OF INTERNATIONAL TRADE AND INDUSTRY (MITI), Japan (1998), "Interim Report by the Study Group on the Impact of Informatisation on Industry", draft, July.

MOWERY, D.C. (ed.) (1996), *The International Computer Software Industry. A Comparative Study of Industry Evolution and Structure*, Oxford University Press.

MOWERY, D.C. (1999), "America's Industrial Resurgence (?): An Overview", in National Research Council, U.S. *Industry in 2000 - Studies in Competitive Performance*, National Academy Press, Washington D.C.

NAGARAJAN A., J.L. BANDER and C.C. WHITE III (1999), "Trucking", in U.S. *Industry in* 2000, Board of Science, Technology and Economic Policy, US National Research Council.

NARIN, F., K.S. HAMILTON, and D. OLIVASTRO (1997), "The Increasing Linkage Between US Technology Policy and Public Science", *Research Policy*, Vol. 26, pp. 317-330.

NATIONAL ASSOCIATION OF BUSINESS ECONOMISTS, http://www.nabe.com.

NATIONAL INSTITUTE OF STANDARDS AND TECHNOLOGY (1998), *The Economics of a Technology-based Services Sector*, Planning Report 98-2, Technology Administration, US Department of Commerce, Washington, DC, January.

NATIONAL INSTITUTE OF STANDARDS AND TECHNOLOGY (1999), *R&D Trends in the U.S. Economy: Strategies and Policy Implications*, Planning Report 99-2, Technology Administration, US Department of Commerce, Washington, DC, April.

NATIONAL OFFICE OF THE INFORMATION ECONOMY (2000), *E-Commerce beyond* 2000, Canberra.

NATIONAL RESEARCH COUNCIL (1998), *Funding a Revolution – Government Support for Computing Research*, Computer Science and Telecommunications Board, Washington, DC.

NATIONAL RESEARCH COUNCIL (1999a), *Securing America's Industrial Strength*, National Academy Press, Washington, DC.

NATIONAL RESEARCH COUNCIL (1999b), *Funding a Revolution*, National Academy Press, Washington, DC.

NATIONAL SCIENCE FOUNDATION (1998a), *Science and Engineering Indicators*, Washington, DC.

NATIONAL SCIENCE FOUNDATION (1998b), "International Mobility of Scientists and Engineers to the United States – Brain Drain or Brain Circulation?", *Issue Brief* NSF 98-316, June.

NATIONAL VENTURE CAPITAL ASSOCIATION (1999), 1999 *Venture Capital Yearbook*, Arlington.

NICOLETTI, G., S. SCARPETTA and O. BOYLAUD (1999), "Summary Indicators of Product Market Legislation with an Extension to Employment Protection Legislation", OECD *Economics Department Working Papers*, No. 226, OECD, Paris.

OECD (1996), *Industry Productivity: International Comparison and Measurement Issues*, OECD Proceedings, OECD, Paris.

OECD (1997a), *Oslo Manual*, OECD, Paris.

OECD (1997b), *Information Technology Outlook* 1997, OECD, Paris.

OECD (1997c), *The OECD Report on Regulatory Reform – Volume II: Thematic Studies*, OECD, Paris.

OECD (1998a), *Technology, Productivity and Job Creation – Best Policy Practices*, OECD, Paris.

OECD (1998b), "Trends and Time Horizons of Research", in *Science, Technology and Industry Outlook* 1998, OECD, Paris.

OECD (1998c), *The Global Research Village: How Information and Communication Technologies Affect the Science System*, OECD, Paris.

OECD (1999a), *OECD Science, Technology and Industry Scoreboard* 1999, OECD, Paris.

OECD (1999b), *Managing Innovation Systems*, OECD, Paris.

OECD (1999c), *Boosting Innovation – The Cluster Approach*, OECD, Paris.

OECD (1999d), *Measuring Globalisation: the Role of Multinationals in* OECD *Economies*, OECD, Paris.

OECD (1999e), *Strategic Business Services*, OECD, Paris.

OECD (1999f), "Mobilising Human Resources for Innovation", DSTI/STP/TIP(99)2/Final, OECD, Paris.

OECD (1999g), *Implementing the* OECD *Jobs Strategy: Assessing Performance and Policy*, OECD, Paris.

OECD (1999h), *The Economic and Social Impact of Electronic Commerce. Preliminary Findings and Research Agenda*, OECD, Paris.

OECD (1999i), *OECD Communications Outlook* 1999, OECD, Paris.

OECD (1999j), "Building Infrastructure Capacity for Electronic Commerce – Leased Line Developments and Pricing", http://www.oecd.org/dsti/sti/it/cm/index.htm, OECD, Paris.

OECD (1999k), *OECD Economic Surveys – Ireland*, OECD, Paris.

OECD (1999l), *Fostering Entrepreneurship*, OECD, Paris.

OECD (2000a), "Innovation and Economic Performance", *Science, Technology and Industry Outlook* 2000, OECD, Paris, forthcoming.

OECD (2000b), "Promoting Innovation and Growth in Services", *Science, Technology and Industry Outlook* 2000, OECD, Paris, forthcoming.

OECD (2000c), *Information Technology Outlook* 2000, OECD, Paris.

OECD (2000d), "Research-based Spin-offs", STI *Review*, No. 26, OECD, Paris, forthcoming.

OECD (2000e), "Benchmarking Industry-Science Relationships", *Science, Technology and Industry Outlook* 2000, OECD, Paris, forthcoming.

OECD (2000f), OECD *Economic Surveys - Finland*, OECD, Paris, forthcoming.

OECD (2000g), "Local Access Pricing and E-commerce", DSTI/ICCP/TISP(2000)1, OECD, Paris.

OECD (2000h), "Cellular Mobile Pricing Structures and Trends", April 2000, http://www.oecd.org/dsti/sti/it/cm/index.htm.

OFFICE OF TECHNOLOGY ASSESSMENT (1995), *Innovation and Commercialization of Emerging Technologies*, Washington, D.C.

OLINER, S.D. and D.E. Sichel (2000), "The Resurgence of Growth in the Late 1990s: Is Information Technology the Story?", Federal Reserve Board, February, mimeo.

PFA RESEARCH (1999), *Pan-European Electronic Commerce and Communications* Survey, Bodmin.

POMP, M. (1998), "Labour Productivity Growth and Low-Paid Work", CPB *Report*, 98/1, The Hague.

PORTER, M.E. (1998), "Clusters and the New Economics of Competition", *Harvard Business Review*, November-December, pp. 77-90.

PRODUCTIVITY COMMISSION (1999), *Microeconomic Reform and Australian Productivity: Exploring the Links*, Research Paper, AusInfo, Canberra.

PYKA, A. (2000), "Informal Networking and Industrial Life Cycles", *Technovation*, Vol. 20.

REARDON, J., R. HASTY and B. COE (1996), "The Effect of Information Technology on Productivity in Retailing", *Journal of Retailing*, Vol. 72, No. 4, pp. 445-461.

RYCROFT, R.W. and D.E. KASH (1999), "Innovation Policy for Complex Technologies", *Issues in Science and Technology*, Autumn.

SALTER, A.J. and B.R. MARTIN (1999), "The Economic Benefits of Publicly Funded Basic Research: A Critical Review", SPRU *Electronic Working Paper Series*, No. 34, Brighton.

SAXENIAN, A.L. (1999), "Silicon Valley's Skilled Immigrants: Generating Jobs and Wealth for California", *Research Brief*, No. 21, Public Policy Institute of California, San Francisco.

SCARPETTA, S., A. BASSANINI, D. PILAT AND P. SCHREYER (2000), "Economic Growth in the OECD Area: Recent Trends at the Aggregate and Sectoral Levels", OECD *Economics Department Working Papers*, OECD, Paris.

SCHREYER, P. (2000), "The Contribution of Information and Communication Technologies to Output Growth", STI *Working Paper* 2000/2, OECD, Paris.

SESSI, Ministère de l'Économie des Finances et de l'Industrie, Secrétariat d'État à l'Industrie (1999), "Technologies de l'information et croissance. Les enseignments d'une simulation", *Les 4 Pages des statistiques industrielles*, No. 116, August.

SHINOZAKI, A. (1999), "An Empirical Analysis of Information-related Investment in Japan and Its Impact on the Japanese Economy", mimeo, Faculty of Economics Kyushu University, Japan, April.

STATISTICS DENMARK AND STATISTICS FINLAND (2000), "Use of ICT in Danish and Finnish Enterprises, 1999", Copenhagen/Helsinki, February.

STIGLITZ, J.E. (1999), "Knowledge in the Modern Economy", in Department of Trade and Industry, *Our Competitive Future – The Economics of the Knowledge Driven Economy*, pp. 37-57, London, December.

STIROH, K. (1999), "Is There a New Economy", *Challenge*, July/August 1999, pp. 82-101.

TAYLOR, P. (1997), "Electronic Revolution in the Retailing World", *The Financial Times*, 3 September.

THOMSON FINANCIAL SECURITIES DATA (2000), *Venture Economics News*, http://www.securitiesdata.com, New Jersey, 7 January.

TRIPLETT, J. (1999), "Economics and Statistics, the New Economy and the Productivity Slowdown", *Business Economics*, April, Vol. 34, No. 2.

TRIPLETT, J.E. and B. BOSWORTH (2000), "Productivity in the Services Sector", paper presented at the meeting of the American Economic Association, January 2000, Boston, Massachusetts, www.Brookings.edu.

TSURU, K. (2000), "Finance and Growth, Some Theoretical Considerations, and a Review of the Empirical Literature", OECD *Economics Department Working Papers*, No. 228, OECD, Paris.

UNITED STATES PATENT AND TRADEMARK OFFICE (USPTO) (2000), "Patent Statistics", www.uspto.gov.

US DEPARTMENT OF COMMERCE (forthcoming), *Digital Economy 2000*, Washington, DC.

WHELAN, K. (2000), "Computers, Obsolescence and Productivity", Federal Reserve Board, February, mimeo.

YOO, K.Y. (2000), "The Role of IT Industry in Korean Economy", Korean Ministry of Finance and Economy, Seoul, mimeo.

OECD PUBLICATIONS, 2, rue André-Pascal, 75775 PARIS CEDEX 16
PRINTED IN FRANCE
(92 2000 03 1 P) ISBN 92-64-17694-2 – No. 51323 2000